The Emperor's Angry Guest

Ralph M. Knox's high school graduation photo, taken two years before he was captured by the Japanese in the Philippines.

The Emperor's Angry Guest

A WORLD WAR II PRISONER OF THE JAPANESE SPEAKS OUT

Ralph M. Knox

Southfarm Press, Publisher
Middletown, Connecticut

Copyright © 1999 by Ralph M. Knox

All rights reserved. No part of this publication may be reproduced or transmitted in any form or by any means, electronic or mechanical, including print, photocopy, recording, or any information storage and retrieval system, without prior written permission from:
SOUTHFARM PRESS, PUBLISHER
Publishing Imprint of Haan Graphic Publishing Services, Ltd.
P.O. Box 1296, Middletown, Connecticut 06457

ISBN: 0-913337-33-1

Library of Congress Cataloging-in-Publication Data
Knox, Ralph M., 1922-
    The emperor's angry guest : a world War II prisoner of the Japanese speaks out / Ralph M. Knox.
        p.   cm.
    Includes bibliographical references and index.
    ISBN 0-913337-33-1
    1. Knox, Ralph M., 1922- . 2. World War, 1939-1945–Prisoners and prisons, Japanese. 3. World War, 1939-1945–Personal narratives, American. 4. Prisoners of war–Japan–Biography. 5. Prisoners of war–United States–Biography. I. Title.
D805.J3K595 1999
940.54'7252–dc21   99-19069
                                                                        CIP

Additional research for *The Emperor's Angry Guest*
by Walter J. Haan, Southfarm Press, Middletown, Connecticut.
Further research concerning the events of May 1942 at Del Monte Field on Mindanao in the Philippines
by Erhard Konerding, Government Documents Librarian, Wesleyan University, Middletown, Connecticut.

Every effort has been made to locate the copyright holders of all copyrighted materials and to secure the necessary permission to reproduce them. In the event of any questions arising as to their use, the publisher will make necessary changes in future printings.

Attention: Schools/Businesses/Veterans Organizations
Southfarm Press Books are available at quantity discounts with bulk purchase for educational, business, or sales promotion use. For information, please write to Special Sales Department at our address shown above.

Visit our website at: http://www.war-books.com

Contents

Introductions 9
My Story 13

PART ONE
1. Beginning of the End 17
2. Life Before the War 19
3. Life in the Military 23
4. Life in the Philippines 27
5. Roosevelt and Churchill 33
6. Preparation for Disaster 39
7. East Wind, Rain 41
8. Clark Field Under Fire 47
9. Destroyed Confidence 57
10. MacArthur and Ike 61
11. Colin P. Kelly, Jr. 67
12. Bataan Bound 71
13. Smell of Defeat 75
14. Manila Envelope 79
15. SS *Mayon* to Mindanao 83
16. Doug Departs 91
17. King Surrenders Bataan 101
18. Doolittle's Raid 109
19. Back at Del Monte 113
20. Fall of Corregidor 117
21. Short End of the Stick 121

PART TWO
22. Count Off 129
23. Hell Ships 133
24. Guests of the Emperor 141
25. The Devil for All 147
26. Sick Bay 155
27. Hospital Camp 159
28. B-29s Firebomb Tokyo 163

29. Hiroshima and Nagasaki   167
30. Stassen the Liberator   173
31. Return to the States   179

PART THREE
32. Back Home Again in Indiana   185
33. Discharged and Deserted   191
34. Return to the Philippines   199
35. Staying Connected   207
36. Looking for Justice   211
37. Misplaced Justice   219
38. Whatever Happened to...   221

PART FOUR: APPENDICES
A. The United States at War:
     Official Report
     By Gen. George C. Marshall   229
B. 28th Bombardment Squadron
     19th Bombardment Group
     May 10, 1942 Roster   239
C. Principal Characteristics
     of Bombers: B-17, B-24,
     B-25, B-29, "Betty"   246
D. Principal Characteristics
     of Pursuits: P-40 and "Zero"   248
E. Death Rates of Allied Prisoners
     of War in the Pacific:
     American, British,
     Australian, and Dutch   250

Bibliography and Sources   253
Index   261
ILLUSTRATION CREDITS
Photographs are courtesy of: Ralph M. Knox,
U.S. Army, U.S. Army Air Corps, U.S. Navy,
U.S. Naval Institute, Defense Department, Boeing,
National Archives, Smithsonian Institution, UPI,
Kansas City Star, Letterman General Hospital

Dedicated to my sisters Alice and Evelyn, and with thanks to God, for my unrelenting faith that sustained me during those dark days

Introductions

A faithful friend is a strong defense: and he that hath found such...hath found a treasure.
Ecclesiasticus 6:14

In *The Emperor's Angry Guest*, Indiana native Ralph M. Knox gives a compelling personal account of his experiences during forty months as a Prisoner of War in World War II. His forthright narrative makes an important contribution to the record of what the war was like for the thousands of American fighting men who suffered at the hands of their Japanese captors. It is a chilling reminder that war is man's most uncivilized undertaking.
RICHARD G. LUGAR, United States Senator

The Emperor's Angry Guest is a moving, vivid account of one man's fight for survival as a prisoner of war in a Japanese camp during World War II. Mr. Knox has led a fascinating life, from his childhood in rural Indiana, to his service in the war, to a successful career in business afterwards. He tells his story with Hoosier honesty and directness.
LEE H. HAMILTON, former Member of Congress
Director, The Center on Congress

The Emperor's Angry Guest is the story of World War Two in the Pacific as seen through the eyes of a plucky young American as a prisoner of war of the Japanese. Ralph M. Knox, along with thousands of other fighting men, suffered untold atrocities as a result of mistakes and miscalculations by government and military officials. Mr. Knox pulls no punches in naming names and in placing the blame, as he saw it, for America's greatest military debacle. With an indomitable spirit, Ralph M. Knox rose above the bungling by high authorities and the Japanese atrocities to survive and enjoy life back in America as a successful businessman and honored citizen.

I served in the same bombardment group with Mr. Knox at the beginning of World War II and was an eyewitness to much of the story he so ably relates.

EDGAR D. WHITCOMB, Governor of Indiana 1969-1973 and author of *Escape From Corregidor*, 1958

The Emperor's Angry Guest is told by a survivor of the death ships and prisoner-of-war camps run by the Japanese during World War II. As the enemy closes in, the reader can feel his anxiety and sense of abandonment by his own government. After he is captured, we experience with him his indomitable will to survive and ultimately the triumph of the human spirit over extreme adversity. Following his liberation, he continued to experience demons created by the unspeakable horror of 40 months as a prisoner of the Japanese war lords.

HUGO C. SONGER, Senior Judge, State of Indiana

The legacy of the gallant defenders of the Philippines and their subsequent mistreatment by the Japanese Armed

Forces while they were prisoners of war will forever be remembered. Ralph Knox and I were a part of that history, having been assigned to the 28th Bomb Squadron at Clark Field in 1941.

The names Bataan and Corregidor become symbols in many minds for something approaching victory. Emotionally, there is a seed of truth in that because the two phases of the war in the Southwest Pacific, the retreat and the return, are keyed in those two names. But actually, for the men involved, the defense was bitter, ugly and humiliating business. The men who took part in it will always bear the scars of humiliation, not only the survivors of the Death March and the prisoner-of-war camps, but the very few who managed to merely delay the Japanese forces. They fought with what they had and did a superior job at it.

This history rests on their spoken word and recollections. To rely so heavily on such a source may not make for definitive history in the eyes of military scholars, yet it may come as close to the truth as possible.

The average reader following the war in the press would never have heard of the 5th Air Base Squadron and its work on Mindanao nor the 200th Coast Artillery unit on Luzon. Nor would they have heard any reference to Corporal Wiezorek. He was executed by a Japanese firing squad along with nine others in a coconut grove near a schoolhouse at Lamban for some small infraction of their rules. There were many others who died on Luzon, on the other islands, and in the Pacific everywhere our war was being fought.

Ralph and I, as citizens of the greatest country in the world, were proud and willing to sacrifice our lives, if necessary, in defense of the freedom it represents.

EDWARD JACKFERT, Past National Commander,
American Defenders of Bataan & Corregidor, Inc.

A recent photo of the author speaking at one of the annual POW Recognition Day observances.

My Story

"words of pain, tones of anger"
Dante, *The Divine Comedy*

I am an ex-POW. I was imprisoned by the Japanese Imperial Army during World War II and, although it happened more than 55 years ago, I'm still angry about it. The commander of the Kawasaki prison camp near Tokyo welcomed my group of starving, mistreated men with words I will never forget: *"You are not prisoners of war. You are guests of the emperor."* He was a lying son of a bitch! I was a prisoner in every sense of the word, and so were thousands of other American soldiers stationed in the Philippine Islands in the 1940s.

Abandoned in a foreign land by our government, we had been surrendered to the enemy by our military leaders in the Philippines. We were sacrificed to the Japanese because we were considered less important than Americans fighting in other parts of the world. For years, we suffered at the hands of the Japanese. The guards beat us viciously, fed us only a small amount of rice each day, and worked us like dogs in Japan's steel mills, mines, and railroad construction projects. Prisoners who became ill or who were severely injured, as I was, received barbaric medical treatment.

I'm angry about that, and I'm angry at those American leaders who allowed it to happen. It was wrong to desert us.

I wrote this book at the encouragement, even insistence, of my sister Alice. She knows my anger. She assumed the process of writing my story would purge the anger from my soul, but it hasn't. The anger is still sharp within my gut. It boils and struggles to flare up nearly every day, as it has since May 10, 1942, the day I was captured.

In this book, I will tell what happened to me before and after I enlisted in the Army in 1940 at the age of 18. And for those who have forgotten, or perhaps have never known the realities of war, I will recount the painful and harrowing experiences that befell the thousands of other young men who fought for our country in the Philippines nearly six decades ago.

In this book, too, I will attempt to dispel heroes, to remind Americans with short memories about our morally weak, militarily inept, and disgustingly callous leaders in the Pacific War. Many of those leaders are remembered today as heroes, but time has been too kind to them. I contend they were ill-prepared, incompetent bastards whose main goals were self-aggrandizement and living the good life. Lies, gross miscalculations of the enemy's power, egregious tactical errors, and bickering among themselves caused pain and suffering to millions of Americans in the 1940s.

PART ONE

Chapter 1
Beginning of the End

> "The miserable have no other medicine but only hope."
> Shakespeare, *Measure for Measure* (III, i, 2)

At 12:40 p.m., Monday, December 8, 1941, sirens began screaming at Clark Field in the Philippines. It was the sound we never wanted to hear but knew was inevitable. In actuality, the sirens came only five and a half hours after Pearl Harbor was attacked, but because of the International Date Line, was Monday for us instead of Sunday. Men ran like hell out of the mess hall and barracks toward their planes or the hangars. They dived into nearby ditches, shallow holes in the ground, or any other makeshift foxhole. Japanese planes were coming in over Mount Pinatubo, heading straight for us at Clark Field. I saw at least three sets of nine planes each in perfect V formations. Historians after the war said there were as many as ninety total Japanese bombers and fighters. I'll take their word for it.

At first men were confused and yelled, "Here comes our Navy!" But as the planes flew closer, I knew it was the Japanese. The rising red sun, just like on the Japanese flag, was painted underneath the wings. I knew I needed to get to my plane, so I cut loose and raced toward the hangar. I didn't make it all the way. Bullets and bombs started falling all around me, tearing up everything. The ground shook like we were having an earthquake. I seemed to be running on Jell-O. With about 15 feet to go, I made a desperate dive for a foxhole. A bomb hit directly behind me, and its concussion pushed me the rest of the way into the hole. The impact pushed another airman in on top of me. He had been running just a few feet behind me. At the exact moment of his desperate leap, he was hit by shrapnel that tore his body at the hips and blew his right arm nearly off. I was covered with his blood and with sand and smoke and the horrible smell of it all. He was dead, and I thought I was dead too.

    I was too scared for anything but a quick peek at the planes droning overhead. The first wave didn't last long, but the damage was devastating. When we were sure the planes had gone, we gingerly climbed out of the ditches and holes and looked around. We saw our friends' faces blackened with smoke, blood oozing from cuts and gashes. Some of our buddies lay motionless in the dirt. Those of us who could move about shook hands with one another or hugged a special friend. We were happy to have survived. It was my first experience with war. I was 19 years old and covered with someone else's blood.

    The Japanese got away unchallenged.

Chapter 2
Life Before the War

> "Dese are de conditions dat prevail."
> Jimmy Durante

I was born May 20, 1922, at Albion, Indiana, to Harry C. and Irene Nowels Knox. My grandfather owned a 640-acre farm half a mile north of Albion on state highway 9. Since Grandpa was a county surveyor, a teacher, and a successful farmer, he was an influential man in the area. I have fond memories of summer visits to his farm with my older brother, Robert. Grandpa went to town every day at noon to get his hot loaf of bread and a sack of candy for us. I can almost taste that candy today. At the summer's end, when it was time for Robert and me to go home to our parents and back to school, Grandpa would take us shopping for a complete wardrobe of new school clothes. We were two of the best dressed boys in school.

On a cold day in March 1935, however, disaster struck the Knox family. One of Grandpa's horses kicked him in the face and he died, two months before my 13th birthday. My father, being the oldest son, was expected to take over the farm, and Robert and I had our hearts set on it. But it didn't happen. My mother and my grandmother didn't get along, never had, and my mother wouldn't set foot on the farm. Grandma blamed my mother for getting herself "in a family way" when she was 16 and forcing my father, 18, to marry her. Because the two women couldn't solve their differences, we had to live elsewhere, sometimes in less than desirable conditions.

My parents raised six children on my father's WPA earnings. The Work Projects Administration was a lifesaver for a lot of poor families back then. The federal agency provided public-works jobs to help relieve unemployment from 1935 to 1943.

We never had much money, so all the Knox kids had to work wherever and whenever we could. During sixth and seventh grades, I was the janitor at our one-room country school. Every day I went to school early, fired up the pot-bellied stove, and had the room warm by the time the teacher rang the starting bell. After school, I swept the wood floor and stoked the stove for the night, all for $2.50 a month. In later summers I worked in the onion fields around Butler, earning ten cents an hour, and picked strawberries for two cents a quart. I mowed yards for a quarter, but not often.

I started high school in 1936 in Butler, Indiana, and played on the varsity baseball, basketball, and track teams. Coach Cletis Jenkins set up stringent rules for all his athletes, and he strictly enforced them. Disobeying Coach's rules was unthinkable. His boys went to bed early, studied hard, and weren't allowed to date. It was just as well. Dating was out of my price range anyway.

Coach Jenkins was like a second father to me. I probably spent more time with him than I did with my own family. My father worked in Fort Wayne and came home only on weekends, and my mother spent a lot of time in Michigan taking care of her mother, who was dying of cancer. Mom took my little sister Evelyn with her, but Alice, a few years older, was taken in by a neighbor. We four boys stayed home to fend for ourselves.

One year, while my mother was gone, I became very ill. It was probably strep throat. There was no one at home to care for me, no medicine and no doctor. I remember being delirious with fever from time to time, but I survived.

My grandmother in Michigan died when I was a senior in high school, and my mother came home for good just a few days before my graduation on May 10, 1940, shortly before my 18th birthday. Our graduation class was small —twenty girls, twenty boys. I wanted to date one of the senior girls, to take her to the graduation ceremony. To do it in style, I felt I needed a car, so I asked the local General Motors dealer, C. J. Maxon, if I could borrow one of his used cars for the day. He said no. I was so dejected I didn't even go to the graduation ceremony.

Because of my athletic ability in high school, I received a scholarship to attend Indiana Central College in Indianapolis. Coach Goode at ICC assigned me to a dormitory and found me a job to help pay my living expenses. I was a busboy at the Marlot Hotel, where I earned $2 a day. I needed more money than that, so the coach got me another job—selling peanuts and soda pop at the Indianapolis Indians baseball games. I still didn't have enough money, so I began to take stock of my situation.

One day as I was walking around downtown Indianapolis and feeling particularly low, I almost bumped into an "Uncle Sam Needs You" poster outside the Army Air Corps recruiting office. Suddenly I was inside talking to the recruiter. It was as if someone had taken hold of me, propelled me through the door, and placed me directly in front of the recruiter's desk.

"Why do you want to pay to go to school," the officer asked, "when I can send you to school and pay you?" It was the best news I had heard in my entire young life! They would pay me $21 a month and feed me too! I enlisted right there on the spot.

Ralph Knox went from making ten cents an hour at home to receiving $21 a month in the Army Air Corps.

Chapter 3
Life in the Military

"Each player on this team—whether he shines in the spotlight of the backfield or eats dirt in the line—must be All-American."

Omar Bradley

The Army Air Corps sent me to Chanute Field for a nine-month crash course in airplane and engine mechanics. Chanute Field was in Rantoul, Illinois, a town much too small for the 10,000 soldiers stationed there. Signs reading "No Dogs or Soldiers Allowed" were plastered on the doors of all the bars in town. I don't think I saw a girl the whole time I was in Rantoul. Their mothers kept them locked up indoors, for good reason. My barracks was close to the classrooms and the huge airplane hangars, where I spent most of my time. I was an attentive student, but boredom and homesickness set in real fast. I hitchhiked back to Butler every chance I got.

One day that winter, President Franklin D. Roosevelt came to visit and relieved our boredom. Thousands of soldiers lined up in formation on the apron in front of the hangars waiting for their hero to arrive. We waited for hours in freezing temperatures and the cold prairie wind. Finally he arrived and spent about 15 minutes reviewing the troops from his 1935 Ford, V-8, four-door convertible with the top down. Roosevelt drove the car even though there were other dignitaries in it. Every soldier went through a short-arm inspection afterward, and those who passed got a three-day pass. I thumbed my way back home to Butler and proudly told everybody there about my close encounter with FDR.

Not long after that, on April 11, 1941, I graduated from airplane mechanics school and was given a choice of what to do next: Stay at Chanute as an instructor (too boring), go to Selfridge Field in Michigan (even more boring), go to Alaska (too cold) or the Panama Canal (too many mosquitoes), or ship off to the Philippine Islands. By this time Hitler was on the rampage. The Nazis had conquered Czechoslovakia, Poland, Denmark, Norway, the Netherlands, Belgium and France. The British were still holding on and everybody knew the war was far from over in Europe. I wanted to get as far away from war, Hitler, and Europe as I possibly could, so I chose the Philippines.

The Army sent me from Illinois to the Philippine Islands by way of New York City. The plan was to transport us from the Brooklyn Navy Yard by ship through the Panama Canal and on west to our destination in the Pacific. My buddies and I were in New York for ten days, free to go anywhere we pleased. One guy was a native New Yorker, and he took a few of us to all the tourist spots. My favorite was the Statue of Liberty. I paid 35 cents to go all the way to the top, and the panoramic view from the crown was worth every penny. Standing up there looking out at the spreading city made me proud to be an American and to be a soldier.

Three of us wound up in Harlem one day, where we

stopped at a bar. After a few drinks, we got cocky and started buying drinks for three young African-American women sitting near us. Suddenly two black men who could have been Joe Louis's cousins marched up to us and demanded, "What are you doing with our women?" Needless to say, we didn't take time to explain what we had in mind. We hit the road.

When it was time to shove off to the Philippines, the Army's plans had changed. We didn't go by ship. They sent us back cross-country by train to San Francisco. The trip took four days and four nights, and it was quite an eye-opener for a young Hoosier like me. When we got to San Francisco I would have slugged anybody who said that this wasn't the best damn country in the world. I had seen with my own eyes the muddy Mississippi, the Rocky Mountains, the Grand Canyon, the prairies, plains and deserts, and I was a proud defender of it all.

We left San Francisco on the passenger ship SS *President Pierce*, a former luxury liner refitted to carry Army troops. On board with us were nurses and civilian pilots heading for China to join General Chennault's Flying Tigers. We slowly sailed away from the pier and passed under the Golden Gate Bridge. Not far away was Alcatraz Island and the federal prison where they kept men who had committed crimes against our country and from whose rock there was no escape. I shuddered, thinking of being confined in such a place.

Once we left the protected waters of the bay and entered the open ocean, heavy waves rolled and rocked the ship and many of us became seasick. After being seasick for 2,400 miles and wanting more than anything to throw up on land instead of on deck, the Hawaii Islands seemed like heaven when they finally came into view. The green, volcanic islands rose from their roots in the sea, forming true gems of the Pacific. We docked at Honolulu, on Oahu, and as we disembarked, beautiful, dark-skinned hula dancers presented us with necklaces fashioned from tropical flowers. We wore our leis like badges of honor. In the middle of town, we drank from a fountain that flowed continuously with pineapple juice. It was delicious and refreshing in the tropical heat, and was produced by Dole, of course. A few steps away, little native boys eight to twelve years old offered us dates with their sisters for 25 cents. We stayed in Honolulu for two days.

The pier at Guam, our next stop for taking on water and other supplies, was not adequate for the *Pierce*, so the captain had to drop anchor 400 to 500 feet offshore. From Guam, we sailed into the South China Sea, into Manila Bay, passing Corregidor and Cavite and docked at Pier 7 in Manila on June 23, 1941. I was about 9,000 miles from home, 7,000 miles from San Francisco, 5,000 miles from Honolulu.

Ralph Knox's 1941 journey to the Philippines started with a cross-country train trip from New York City to San Francisco.

Chapter 4
Life in the Philippines

"I wish the novelists who write about the islands...would say a little more about the heat and perspiration...."
Viscount Northcliffe, *My Journey Round the World*, 1923

We disembarked from the *President Pierce* on July 4, loaded down with our personal belongings and stepped sharply onto our new Philippine home, Luzon Island. At one time, Teddy Roosevelt had called the Philippines America's "Achilles heel." We'd soon learn why.

Army buses, some with standing room only, left for Cavite Navy Base, Nichols Field, Fort McKinley, Subic Bay, Corregidor, Cebu and other exotic places. My bus went to Clark Field, 65 miles north of Manila. There were 50 of us.

What a sorry sight Clark Field was. To get there, we had traveled a narrow winding, gravel road cut through tangled jungle growth. The base itself was shockingly crude for an air base. It was in a clearing, with mountains off in the distance. All the buildings were constructed of wood—the barracks, the mess hall, the hangars, everything. It was vintage World War I. Even the planes were antiquated, and the runways the planes took off from and landed on were gravel, not tarmac.

First Sergeant Kristopolis greeted us. The tall, no-nonsense NCO of the 28th bomb squadron took us to the quartermaster at Fort Stotsenburg for our khaki uniforms, underwear, shoes and accessories. Each of us got a .45-caliber automatic pistol, several clips of ammunition, and a mosquito net, which turned out to be the most useful gift of all. It would be a barrier to the swarms of disease-carrying mosquitoes, flying cockroaches and several species of bats native to the tropics.

Fort Stotsenburg, less than a mile from Clark Field, was Clark's rich cousin. Gleaming white stucco buildings sparkled in the tropical sun, giving the compound a British military look. Stotsenburg housed the cavalry and a few other elite installations. A well-kept polo field separated Fort Stotsenburg from its poorer relative.

I was assigned to a twin-engine B-18A bomber, one of 18 such planes stationed at Clark Field. We also had 12 Martin B-10A bombers and a few P-40 pursuit planes. Several guys who had trained with me at Chanute Field in Illinois were assigned to the same squadron: Eddy Jackfert, Robert Call, "Shorty" Martin, Marshall Lieb, and Eugene Lange. I was glad to have them around, to see their familiar faces in such a foreign land.

My job was to do the pre-flight work on the B-18, refuel it and make sure all the instruments worked. The pilot, First Lieutenant Harold "Red" Fischer, took me and the other crew members on long flights to such exotic places as New Guinea, Celebes, Borneo, and Sumatra. Those flights not only provided valuable training for us, they insured that we accrued enough flying time to collect flight pay. After we were airborne in the "flying coffin," which we nicknamed the B-18s, Red would often allow crew members to take turns manning the controls to fly the plane.

Down on the ground, when we weren't pampering the planes, we spent hours and hours riding the horses at Fort Stotsenburg. We traded long rides in our B-18s for half days with the horses. There was no better way for a country boy from Indiana to spend his time.

Clark Field was a plum assignment in those days. The weather was wonderful all the time. Flocks of colorful birds—parrots, canaries, and parakeets—chirped and flitted about in the heavy tropical vegetation west of the base. Tall palms and banana trees with broad, dark-green leaves shaded our walkways. Not one man had to pull KP, make beds, wash clothes, or even shine his own shoes. Filipino boys did everything. Each soldier pitched in a peso or two to pay the boys' wages. The mess hall was always open, and it served hearty meals. You could order anything you wanted to eat anytime you wanted to eat it. Bacon and eggs at midnight. Fresh banana or coconut cream pie for breakfast, lunch or dinner. Day or night, cool tropical drinks quenched our thirst. We were living in a tropical paradise. No wonder so many old-timers were at Clark. It was like a perpetual vacation.

The little village of Angeles was just outside Clark Field, and we made a beeline there whenever we got a pass. Angeles had one small bar that served up cheap beer and rum and coke, and a jukebox that played "Rose of San Antonio" nonstop. Pretty Filipino girls hung out at the bar and were ready and willing to lead a soldier upstairs for a quickie whenever he was willing to shell out two pesos, about a dollar in American money. The big price came later, however, when the soldier had to go through the prophylactic station set up at Clark's entrance gate. Nobody got through that gate without getting a shot to ward off venereal diseases. God! It was like shooting iodine up your penis.

Single non-commissioned officers of staff sergeant rank and above were provided a free Filipino girl and a hut off base for the NCO and his girl to set up house. The typical hut provided was on stilts to keep its floor dry during the rainy season. Dogs made their homes under these huts.

Hikes to Mount Pinatubo were popular ways to while away the time when we weren't raising hell in Angeles or riding horses at Stotsenburg. We'd walk up to the volcano's base and sneak around in the thick vegetation, hoping to catch a glimpse of the native headhunters and Pygmies. Pinatubo was dormant at the time, so we didn't worry about eruptions. The adult Pygmies we saw were only about 3 feet tall and carried 6-foot-long spears, quite a novelty for a young boy from northern Indiana. Clark's old-timers told us stories about the headhunters sneaking into the base at night to scavenge the garbage dumps or anything left out in the open, so we were very careful not to venture out alone in the dark or leave valuables lying around.

Not only did the Filipino headhunters unnerve us, the snakes slithering through the trees and underbrush jostled our nerves too. One night a guy shot and killed a 5-foot-long baby python and hid it in the cot of a fellow soldier who was away on an evening pass to Angeles. The guy returned to base more drunk than sober and unknowingly crawled into bed with the snake. When he awoke the next morning and saw the thing next to him, he went berserk—jumped out of bed, grabbed his .45 and emptied it into the bed and everything around it. Thank God he didn't kill anybody. The soldier who pulled the malicious trick was deservedly court-martialed, and we all learned to check our beds for snakes before jumping in.

Mail arrived and went out once a month on the *China Clipper*. In early November 1941, I unknowingly sent my last letter home. "Mother," I predicted, "by the time you receive this letter, we will be at war with Japan." My prediction was based on radio news reports and talk among the soldiers of agreements being made between President Franklin Roosevelt and British Prime Minister Winston Churchill, and the threat by Secretary of State Cordell Hull that the Japanese "get out of French Indochina or else."

About this time, Colonel Eugene Eubank and several pilots under his command flew thirty-five B-17s, six of them B-17Cs along with 29 B-17Ds, from San Francisco to Hawaii and then on to the Philippines. At that time it was the greatest mass flight in aviation history. What a beautiful sight those four-engined silver birds were compared to our B-18s and the obsolete B-10s.

Upon arrival, Colonel Eubank took command of the 28th Bombardment Squadron, one of three squadrons in the 19th Bombardment Group. Colonel Lester J. Maitland, our previous commander, was still around but was drunk most of the time. Usually on Sundays Maitland would borrow a horse from the fort and pull an inspection tour of the men at Clark Field. One Sunday, Maitland actually fell off his horse and landed on his ass right in front of us. A couple of the men helped him climb back up into the saddle, and he went on his merry way. On an earlier occasion, Maitland had issued an order for all personnel at Clark Field to stop shaving and to grow a beard! We became known as the "Hair" Corps of the Philippines. The order didn't affect me much. I was so young only peach fuzz grew on my face anyway.

I wasn't to know it at the time, but one order of Maitland's probably saved many lives. Maitland had ordered trenches to be dug on Clark Field for personnel to dive into if the base ever came under air attack. I later learned the pursuit pilots called the trenches "Maitland's Folly" until December 8th when they all had to dive into them.

None of Clark's old-timers had technical experience on the new B-17s that Colonel Eubank brought in, so for the most part, it was up to me and the other recent Chanute graduates to keep the planes in flying condition. I was promoted to Sergeant because I was assigned as Crew Chief for one of the B-17s. I replaced Staff Sergeant Jeffries, who was restricted to base because he had a venereal disease. Jeffries, who was in his thirties, and the other old-timers seemed happy to give up B-17 maintenance duty and were counting the days before they were to go home.

Clark Field in the Philippines, as it appeared in 1941. Fort Stotsenburg was in the upper center, next to the foothills of the Zambales Mountains. The rectangular, tree-lined area was the parade ground.

Chapter 5
Roosevelt and Churchill

"The partnership that saved the west
and sacrificed the east."
Ralph M. Knox

As far back as January 1939, President Franklin Roosevelt had called for "measures short of war" to defeat aggressors. To American mothers and fathers, he gave his solemn pledge that "your boys are not going to be sent into foreign wars."

When war broke out in Europe in September 1939, Roosevelt's course of action was well determined. The Western Hemisphere's neutrality zone was created. The Act of Havana turned the Monroe Doctrine Defense into a Pan-American pact.

Roosevelt continued to take decisive action after the German victories in Norway, Denmark, the Netherlands, Belgium, and France. He persuaded Congress to allow "cash-and-carry" purchasing of arms by the Allies. Prime Minister Churchill persuaded Roosevelt that Britain came first, that the real enemy was Hitler. In September 1940, the United

States sent fifty aged destroyers to England in exchange for 99-year leases on naval and air bases in the Caribbean and Newfoundland. The following month, selective service became law. A new army was drafted. In March 1941, the multi-billion-dollar Lend-Lease program for Great Britain was inaugurated. On May 27, just a few months after his third term began, Roosevelt declared an "unlimited national emergency."

The success of Hitler's armies in Europe prompted Roosevelt to speed up defense production, ask Congress for new billions, and call out the National Guard for Army training. Roosevelt and Churchill met aboard the British battleship *Prince of Wales* off the coast of Newfoundland in August 1941. Churchill stressed the Nazi menace to the U.S. and the Atlantic Charter resulted from those meetings.

President Roosevelt had initiated the meetings with Churchill. He thought it would be a good idea to lay down certain guidelines and policies in a drawn-up joint declaration of the course of action to follow during the next few years. Shortly thereafter, the United States found itself closer and closer to war.

Japanese-American relations were deteriorating. The Japanese were feeling the pinch of the July 1941 U.S., Dutch and British embargo against them. They needed the oil, scrap iron, rubber and other essentials being embargoed.

The Atlantic picture also gave Roosevelt concern. Attacks on the Atlantic shipping lanes increased. In early September 1941, a German sub attacked the American destroyer, *Greer*, off Iceland, and Roosevelt ordered the U. S. Navy to sink German submarines on sight and to escort British convoys. Later that month, German U-boats torpedoed the American destroyers *Kearny* and *Reuben James*, sinking the *Reuben James* and killing 115 of the men aboard.

In his September 11, 1941, Fireside Chat on the radio, Roosevelt had exclaimed, "When you see a rattlesnake poised to strike, you do not wait until he has struck before you crush him." He particularly had the Germans in mind.

In early October, Roosevelt asked Congress to rescind the Neutrality Act so as to arm American merchant ships.

In the following months, negotiations between Secretary of State Cordell Hull and Japanese Ambassador Kichisaburo Nomura in Washington, D.C., failed. Finally, Japan sent a veteran diplomat, Saburo Kurusu, to Washington to assist Nomura, and between them, Japan offered a settlement on November 20, 1941. It required that the U.S. withdraw aid to China, unfreeze Japanese assets, and furnish Japan with unlimited oil. In return, Japan would not send further troops into the Pacific, except for French Indochina. Secretary Hull refused those terms and ordered the Japanese to get out of French Indochina. By November 24, 1941, Roosevelt had speculated to his Cabinet that the U.S. would be attacked by the Japanese within a week and cabled Churchill to be "prepared for real trouble."

Lieutenant General Walter Short, the Garrison Commander in Hawaii, and Admiral Husband E. Kimmel, the Pacific Fleet Commander-in-Chief, were warned of an aggressive action to begin in a few days. But Kimmel expected Japan to attack the Philippines, not Pearl Harbor.

On November 3, 1941, Major General Lewis H. Brereton arrived in Manila to assume command of the Far East Air Forces (FEAF) at the request of General Douglas MacArthur.

Brereton had been concerned that the presence of

strong, unprotected B-17 Flying Fortress bombardment units in the Philippines might goad an aggressive enemy such as the Japanese to launch an air attack. But the War Department and General MacArthur were both of the opinion that hostilities wouldn't break out in the Philippines before April 1, 1942.

MacArthur, after reading a letter marked "For the Eyes of General MacArthur Only" from the Chief of Staff, General George Marshall, that Brereton had brought with him, jumped up from his desk and threw his arms around Brereton. Turning to Richard Sutherland, his Chief of Staff in Manila, MacArther exclaimed, "Dick, they are going to give us everything we have asked for." But it wasn't going to be nearly fast enough.

At the end of November 1941, General Marshall summarized for the Secretary of War the air reinforcements already shipped or scheduled for shipment to the Philippines:

35 B-17s:	already in the Philippines
52 A-24s:	due in the Philippines November 30, 1941 (They never arrived)
50 P-40s:	Pursuits already in the Philippines
64 P-40s:	(total) had been shipped from the west coast on October 19 and November 9, 1941.

From November 30 to December 6, 1941, a Japanese strike force commanded by Admiral Yamamoto, sailed east, north of the Pacific shipping lanes, with six carriers in three columns, flanked by battleships and cruisers. The U.S. Naval Governor at Guam ordered all its classified material to be destroyed. On December 6, 1941, Admiral Yamamoto's invasion force was only 600 miles from the Hawaiian Islands.

Fortunately, the American aircraft carrier *Lexington* wasn't at Pearl Harbor. It was en route to Wake Island, ferrying Marine aircraft for a bomber flight that was due there in a couple of days.

Roosevelt's Pacific rattlesnake was about to strike. He had recognized it long ago, baited it, antagonized it, but did not do enough to crush it. He needed this snakebite to rally the American people to fight the Axis powers, starting with Germany. Churchill was depending on an attack on the U.S., such as the one at Pearl Harbor, to obtain U.S. military support in Europe against Nazi Germany. The Germans had no immediate plans to declare war on the U.S. in 1941, but the Japanese took the bait.

My life in the Philippines was about to take a dramatic turn.

These two photos of the B-17 illustrate the visual difference between the earlier models, such as the B-17C and B-17D, and the later versions, starting with the B-17E. The top photo shows a B-17D; the bottom photo shows a later model. Note that the tail of the B-17D is smaller than on the aircraft in the bottom photo.

Chapter 6
Preparation for Disaster

> "My theory of getting as far away from war, Europe and Hitler...was about to come up and bite me in the ass."
> Ralph M. Knox

I was assigned as crew chief to one of the new seventeen B-17s left on Clark Field. Because of my new assignment, I was promoted to Sergeant, the proper rank of a crew chief.

On December 5th, fifteen of our B-17 Flying Fortresses had been flown south to the new makeshift base at Del Monte Field on Mindanao, the second-largest Philippine island. Officers thought the planes would be safer there from enemy attack. Del Monte was 500 miles south of Clark Field and out of range of Japanese land-based bombers flying in from Formosa. Fifteen hundred men had worked for two weeks at the Del Monte pineapple plantation upgrading the company's small airstrip into a runway a mile long and capable of handling the big heavy bombers.

MacArthur had actually ordered Major General Lewis H. Brereton to move all thirty-five B-17s from Clark Field to the Del Monte plantation airfield, but for reasons still not entirely clear, Brereton did not completely carry out the order.

Our flying time accelerated. Unidentified aircraft had been sighted near Clark Field on December 1. The next morning at dawn a Japanese reconnaissance plane was spotted over Clark and radar detected other planes off the Luzon coast. One colonel guessed they were getting their range data fixed from a possible rendezvous site in Formosa.

The war that was sure to come was all we talked about at the base. We were on constant alert and wore our .45 automatic pistols at all times. Our planes were guarded round-the-clock. No passes were issued. We yearned for the little bar in Angeles that we could no longer frequent and for the pretty Filipino girls now off limits. My theory of getting as far away from war, Europe, and Hitler as possible was about to come up and bite me in the ass.

Meanwhile, we continued to park our aircraft in neat rows as per orders.

Chapter 7
East Wind, Rain

"The go signal for attack on the
United States was *East Wind, Rain*"
Brigadier General Elliott R. Thorpe

Brigadier General Elliott R. Thorpe, in his 1969 book, *East Wind, Rain*, felt that his biggest contribution to the war effort as an army intelligence officer was to cable Washington from Java in the Netherlands East Indies about the forthcoming attack on Hawaii. Thorpe had sent four warning messages, but could find only one in the records of the Congressional Pearl Harbor Investigation. He sent that warning on December 5th, which was December 4th in Washington. To his dismay, Thorpe found that his warnings were not taken seriously.

The commander in chief of the Dutch army, Major General Hein ter Poorten, had personally provided Thorpe with dispatches that outlined the coming attacks on Hawaii, the Philippines, Malaya and Thailand. The Dutch had broken the official Japanese code and were recording daily the Japanese messages going and coming from all over the

Pacific as the Japanese preparations for war were finalized.

The Japanese wanted all their fleets in the proper positions when the final attack signal was broadcast. Because the weather at sea was unpredictable and they wanted their attacks to be simultaneous, the actual "go" signal would come from Tokyo in the form of a weather broadcast.

After the attack on Pearl Harbor, this became known as the "Winds" message in the discussions of what went wrong. The go signal for their surprise attack on the U.S. was "East Wind, Rain," just as Thorpe had warned.

Back at Hawaii, the U.S. Navy consisted of eight battleships, three cruisers, sixteen destroyers, and numerous smaller ships such as minelayers—all neatly arranged as sitting ducks in the harbor. Everything was ready for President Roosevelt's hoped-for snakebite or first strike by the Axis.

Despite Intelligence warnings, such as that of General Thorpe's, of a possible attack by the Japanese, the high-level officers on Hawaii and in the Philippines seemed to not grasp the situation.

General Douglas MacArthur and Admiral Thomas C. Hart and their staffs in the Philippines had no excuses. Formosa, less than 500 miles north of Manila, was the base for the Japanese Imperial Navy's IIth Air Fleet, as shown by numerous American reconnaissance flights. Clark Field, Manila and Bataan were all within bombing and strafing range from the Japanese fortified island.

In the early hours of December 7, 1941, the Japanese attack force was some 200 miles from Oahu, refueling and loading bombs on their six aircraft carriers plowing toward Hawaii. At about 6:30 a.m., from 90 miles away, the first wave of 183 Japanese aircraft—49 bombers and 40 torpedo bombers escorted by 45 Zero fighters—took off for the attack. At 7:00, a U.S. antisubmarine patrol crew sighted several Japanese subs and fired depth charges. A PBY depth-charged another contact. Hickam Field, the Army base south of Pearl Harbor, had shut down its radar for breakfast. Fort Shafter was alerted but responded, "Don't worry, it's probably our B-17s coming in from San Francisco."

At 7:56 a.m., December 7, 1941, the first wave of 18 dive bombers hit Hickam Field at Pearl Harbor, where our fighters and bombers were parked, row after row, in perfect formation. The Japanese bombers destroyed our PBY flying boats and ramps on Ford Island, home of the Naval Control Center.

At 7:57, the raid exploded with such fury that the first few minutes caught everyone by surprise. Sailors were in the act of hoisting the colors on the fantails of their respective ships. Gunfire burst out, church bells rang, bombs screamed, and torpedoes exploded. The *Nevada, Arizona, Oklahoma,* and *West Virginia* were hit. The *Maryland* and the *Tennessee* were hit, but less severely damaged. The *California* was the last of the battleships to be hit.

At 8:30 a.m., Admiral Kimmel, commander of Pacific Fleet forces at Pearl, contacted Secretary of the Navy Frank Knox in D.C., reporting the devastating raid on Pearl Harbor. Knox replied, "This can't be true. You must mean the Philippines."

In the lull before the second attack, twelve of our B-17s coming in from the States, low on fuel, were told to land wherever they could. Minutes later, the second wave of 86 Japanese dive bombers, 54 low-flying bombers, and 36 fighters hit. In all, 360 planes and six Japanese carriers were involved in this devastating raid, killing 2,400 Americans.

Hawaii lost 190 planes on the ground, and another 160 were damaged. Eighteen warships were either sunk or damaged beyond repair. Later that day, Secretary Knox, Secretary Hull, Admiral Stark, General Marshall, and Secretary of War Stimson gathered with President Roosevelt at the White House. Roosevelt issued several orders: Guard all factories and military installations. Ground all private planes. Silence all amateur radios. Round up all Japanese aliens. Roosevelt spoke with Churchill. They agreed to make simultaneous declarations of war the next day, December 8.

At Shanghai, China, our gunboat *Wake* was seized by the Japanese and renamed the *Tatara*.

Back in the Philippines, depending on which source you believe, MacArthur had been notified of the attack on Pearl Harbor at around midnight, or 3 a.m. or 4 a.m., Philippine time, which is several hours ahead of Hawaii. MacArthur claimed to have been notified at 3 a.m.

Major General Lewis H. Brereton wanted to send his B-17s at once to bomb Formosa, but MacArthur was indecisive. The shock of events had MacArthur so confused that his thinking was paralyzed. He felt that he could not attack the Japanese or give Brereton permission to bomb Formosa because no declaration of war existed, even though Japan had attacked Pearl Harbor just a few hours before. His staff also knew that, as early as 6:00 a.m. on December 8 (Philippine time), Japanese planes had bombed the seaplane tender *William B. Preston*, anchored in the Gulf of Davao off Mindanao Island.

The Philippines might have been saved if General Brereton's request for a preemptive bombing strike on Formosa had been carried out. At the very least, Brereton's planned bombing of Formosa would have provided valuable time for reinforcing our Philippine forces. And our B-17s wouldn't have been sitting in neat rows awaiting their destruction.

Simultaneously, audacious attacks were being carried out by the Japanese on Singapore, Guam, Wake Island and Hong Kong. The garrison on Guam consisted of 500 sailors and marines with nothing but machine guns and pistols. About 100 American construction workers were also on Guam. The USS *Penguin* was sunk, leaving only two old patrol craft in the "Guam Navy." At Wake, 36 Japanese bombers flying from Roi in the Marshall Islands destroyed seven of Wake's fighters and large gasoline storage tanks. The first hostile Japanese action at Hong Kong was a large air raid on Kai Tak airfield on the morning of December 8th.

Tending our B-17 sitting ducks at Clark Field on December 8th, my buddies and I were about to experience a similar hell.

A destroyed B-17 rests near Hangar Number Five, Hickam Field, following the December 7, 1941, attack by Japanese aircraft.

As seen from a Japanese plane participating in the attack on Pearl Harbor, planes and hangars burn at Wheeler Army Air Field.

Chapter 8
Clark Field Under Fire

"Here comes our Navy!"
Shouts by confused soldiers and airmen
as Japanese planes were coming in
over Mount Pinatubo

I was sleeping in the wee hours of the morning of December 8, 1941 (the 7th in Hawaii because of the international date line). Suddenly a rude hand shook my shoulder. It was Shorty Martin. Some of the men had just returned from a party off-base and were feeling their rum and Coca Colas.

"Wake up, Ralph! Wake up!" Shorty exclaimed. "Big news—Pearl Harbor's been attacked."

News trickled in after that about heavy damages and casualties. It was hard to comprehend that it was really happening, even though many of us had felt that Roosevelt and Churchill would lead us eventually to this day. I thought of the letter I had sent home in November predicting war.

By 4 a.m., we air corpsmen had gathered in the mess hall to get orders on what equipment we should have and what we should do. By daylight, I was lugging around 10 clips of ammo for my .45-caliber pistol, a gas mask, and a few emergency rations. By 6 a.m., all combat crews had been ordered down to the hangars. Tanks were surrounding the field, antiaircraft gunners were on the alert, and noncombat personnel were assigned to machine-gun posts.

After breakfast, I checked the flight board to see if my plane was scheduled to fly. It was. At 8:30 we would take off on a reconnaissance patrol. Almost immediately we learned that General Brereton's request to bomb Formosa early that morning had been denied. Confusion tainted the air inside and outside the hangar. Crews stood around shifting their feet, waiting for the final word. Would we load up with bombs or what? Apparently Brereton was still trying to get MacArthur's permission to bomb Formosa. But finally word came down for Brereton to return to his headquarters at Neilson Field and await further orders. We would not fly a bombing run. Colonel Eubank directed us to go ahead with our normal 8:30 reconnaissance mission, and as crew chief, I prepped my plane and readied it for takeoff.

Captain Harold "Red" Fischer, the C.O. of my bomber, taxied the plane onto the runway. Two other B-17s lined up behind us, ready to follow us into the air. Equipped with cameras, they would photograph our mission. Fischer suddenly called his entire crew—me, the navigator, the bombardier, the radio man, and two gunners—up to the cockpit for a lecture. "Well, men," he said, including his co-pilot in the group, "it looks like we're at war whether we want to be or not. I know nothing more about what's what than you do. I've heard only what you've heard. My instructions are as follows: We will fly this morning's recon without bombs and scout around for any massed troop convoys. We'll fly around the coast from Iba, north to Aparri and out to sea toward Formosa. If we run into the enemy, we'll take all precautions to avoid them and return to Clark the fastest and best way we can. Under no circumstances will we fire on the Japanese. MacArthur has a hang-up about the fact that war hasn't been declared. If we get shot down, we'll get everything out of this bird that we can. First, the bombsight goes, then the maps. If we're forced down in an area where the Japanese are, destroy the bombsight first, then burn the plane if possible. You're all young men, some married with wives and children back home, others have sweethearts and families. All I can say is that we can't think about them now. We've got a job before us now. May God be with us all. Now, let's go."

Those were my first instructions of war. God! The biggest game in the world was about to begin and I was a participant, not a spectator.

With all four engines revved to the hilt and permission from the tower, Captain Fischer headed the big bomber down the long gravel taxiway. At 2,100 rpms, he released the brakes, pulled back on the wheel, and we were up and away. It was about 8:45 a.m.

After Iba, we followed the coastline up through San Fernando then farther north over Vigan and swung around to Aparri. Cloud cover was heavy. Occasional breaks revealed the choppy water below. Nothing seemed amiss, but we kept in constant radio contact with Clark. Suddenly a large gap appeared in the clouds, and there it was—a huge Japanese task force of about 80 ships, and it was headed directly for Batan Island. Batan Island is about 150 miles south of Formosa and 150 miles north of the Philippines. We circled the task force several times, allowing the photo planes time to get their pictures. We had seen the enemy and had taken their picture!

I said my first war-time prayer.

When we radioed our encounter to Clark Field, Eubank ordered us to get the hell out of there as fast as we could. He thought Japanese fighters might attack us. Our return route took us southwest. We skirted the northern part of Luzon, west of Aparri, Vigan, and San Fernando, and we saw two other Japanese task forces. One was headed straight for Aparri; the other had a bead on Vigan.

I was sure Eubank would order us to load up with bombs and return to knock the hell out of the Japanese, but he didn't. We got back to base about 11:15 a.m., and the following happened almost too quickly to record.

First, all U.S. planes in the air over the Philippines were ordered back to their respective fields to await further orders. All Clark's planes were back on the field by noon.

Second, Don Bell, a news announcer in Manila, broadcast that Clark Field and Baguio were under attack. We never found out the circumstances of that premature news broadcast.

Third, most of the airmen on the ground and the crews from the returning planes headed to the mess hall for an early lunch.

Fourth, after the recon photos were developed, a call was made to General Lewis H. Brereton, who then contacted MacArthur. MacArthur finally handed down the order to refuel the B-17s, load them with bombs, and wait. He would give the final order to bomb Formosa sometime in the afternoon. Later it was learned that General Hap Arnold telephoned MacArthur from the United States, telling him not to get caught with the bombers on the ground like Pearl Harbor!

Fifth, we learned that the Japanese launched three

other task forces besides the three that our crew sighted and sent one each to Legaspi, Davao, and the Jolo Islands.

Sixth, the P-40 fighter planes that had been patrolling the South China Sea were back home and refueling. At Nichols Field, the 17th Pursuit Squadron, which was covering Clark Field, also landed to refuel. The Third and 34th Pursuit Squadrons were on the ground, standing by at Iba and Del Carmen.

At 12:40 p.m., December 8, 1941, sirens began screaming at Clark Field. It was the sound we never wanted to hear but knew was inevitable. Men ran like hell out of the mess hall and barracks toward their planes or the hangars. They dived into ditches, shallow holes in the ground or any makeshift foxhole. Japanese planes were coming in over Mount Pinatubo, heading straight for us at Clark Field. I saw at least three sets of nine planes in perfect V formations. Historians after the war said there were as many as 90 total Japanese bombers and fighters.

At first, men were confused and yelled, "Here comes our Navy!" But as the planes flew closer, I knew it was the Japanese. The rising red sun, just like on the Japanese flag, was painted underneath the wings. I knew I needed to get to my plane, so I cut loose and raced toward the hangar. I didn't make it all the way. Bullets and bombs started falling all around me, tearing up everything. The ground shook like we were having an earthquake or we were running on Jell-O. With about 15 feet to go, I made a desperate dive for a foxhole. A bomb hit directly behind me, and its concussion pushed me the rest of the way into the hole. The impact pushed another airman in on top of me. He had been running just a few feet behind me. At the exact moment of his desperate leap, he was hit by shrapnel that tore his body at the hips and blew his right arm nearly off. I was covered with his blood and with sand and smoke and the horrible smell of it all. He was dead, and I thought I was dead too.

I was too scared for anything but a quick peek at the planes droning overhead. The first wave didn't last long, but the damage was devastating. When we were sure the planes had gone, we gingerly climbed out of the ditches and holes and looked around. We saw our friends' faces blackened with smoke and blood oozing from cuts and gashes. Some of our buddies lay motionless in the dirt. Those of us who could move about shook hands with one another or hugged a special friend. We were happy to have survived. It was my first experience with war. I was 19 years old and covered with someone else's blood.

The Japanese got away unchallenged. Their bombers did their dirty work from an altitude of 22,000 to 25,000 feet, while our antiaircraft guns, manned by the 200th Coast Artillery at Fort Stotsenburg, had a maximum range of only about 22,000 feet. In addition, most of the Coast Artillery's ammunition was manufactured in 1932. Over half the shells were duds, their fuses corroded by age and the tropical heat and humidity.

Fifteen minutes later, here came the Japanese again. As the planes were approaching, Colonel Eubank was standing out in the open taking motion pictures. Planes were strafing directly toward him. Instinctively, I made a tackle dive, knocking him to the ground. We crawled together into a culvert that went through an embankment. We watched as three new waves of Japanese planes strafed everything in sight, fuel dumps, planes, anything left standing. Our own ammunition dump exploded in a barrage of fireworks. It sounded exactly like the Fourth of July back home. Eubank and I covered our heads.

The attack on Iba was just as devastating. The Japanese hit them with 54 bombers and 50 pursuits. All but two of the Third Squadron's P-40s were lost.

America's Far East Air Force was cut in half. The planes had been sitting ducks lined up on the ground.

Several pilots at Clark Field had tried desperately to reach their planes during the raid. Many were riddled with bullets en route and others were burned alive sitting in their cockpits trying to take off. The very few who managed to get off the ground were unable to offer much help.

Our barracks were demolished and smoldering. We heard men calling for help, saw men whose limbs had been blown off, men with large holes in their head or their torso, some with blood dripping from their mouth. We helped the ones we could. Some of the bodies were burned beyond recognition and swollen twice their size. Their clothes had been burned off and their bones lay naked to the world.

One group of eight men died a horrible death on a gasoline truck. The truck was fully loaded with 50-gallon drums of fuel for the P-40s. Several of the men were riding on top of the truck, a common practice. One of the Japanese' bombs made a direct hit on the truck, which exploded in a fiery mass. The men's charred, dismembered bodies were scattered all round the truck.

The sight and stench of death were almost unbearable, yet many young men performed glorious acts of courage. I saw soldiers trying to carry their wounded buddies all the way to Fort Stotsenburg, nearly a mile. They were under air attack the whole way.

Miracles happened that day too, depending on where you were and your luck. One master sergeant was working on a B-17 when the first wave of Japanese bombers came over. When the bombs began to drop, he high-tailed it toward the hangar across the runway. Midway across, he was knocked to the ground by the impact and he lay there flat on his stomach throughout the whole raid. When it was over, he discovered that the entire back of his shirt had been ripped off by flying shrapnel, but otherwise he didn't have a scratch on him.

A Chinese man and his daughter, however, met a different fate. They had set up a small concession stand right outside our barracks to sell us soft drinks, beer, and candy. When the raid began, both of them scrambled into a foxhole, but suddenly the old man remembered he'd left the cash box behind. Both of them went to get it. Just as the two entered the stand, a bomb hit it and they were blown to bits. The cash box might have contained 30 pesos at most.

A good friend of mine, Robert Call, pulled an unbelievably daring stunt during the initial raid on December 8. He had just finished putting a new engine in a B-18 and was bringing it out of the hangar. As he taxied the plane, he saw the Japanese coming and realized what was happening, so he revved up the engines and took off all by himself. The Japanese took up the chase, but somehow he got away from them and was able to land a few miles away at one of our emergency landing fields. Robert wasn't even a pilot! He and I were classmates at aircraft engine school at Chanute Field in Illinois.

Nichols Field was attacked at midnight of that first day of war. Captain E. L. Sackett of the U.S. Navy was able to observe that night attack from the USS *Canopus*, an old submarine tender stationed at Cavite Navy Yard. He described the night attack on Nichols:

"From our anchorage off Cavite, just far enough away to muffle the noise, the showers of red and yellow tracer bullets, the sparklers of anti-aircraft bursts followed by the bonfire glare of burning hangars and planes had an unreal quality which made it hard to realize that this was war, and our own countrymen were fighting and dying amidst the conflagration."

But Americans were fighting and dying. Sackett reported that Philippine fifth columnists had led the Japanese bombers unerringly to their target by bracketing the field with flares. A brilliant moon didn't help the defenders at Nichols either.

There were 12 obsolete B-10A bombers at Clark Field
in the Philippines when Ralph M. Knox arrived in 1941.
The B-10 was the first bomber to have an enclosed
gunner's cockpit. The Dutch air forces in the Far East
also had the obsolete B-10 when the Japanese attacked.
Using 12 B-10s, the Dutch sank 26 enemy ships before
their B-10s were destroyed on the ground by enemy bombing.

Chapter 9
Destroyed Confidence

"We rummaged through the ashes and rubble like scavengers."
Ralph M. Knox

When it was all over, we straggled back to our bombed-out barracks, like people returning to the ruins of their tornado-damaged home. We rummaged through the ashes and rubble like scavengers. What else could we do?

The Japanese destroyed more than the wood and glass of the barracks. They destroyed our security, our confidence, as well as everything that constituted our home away from home. Our personal belongings were gone, even our service records that were stored in the first sergeant's office on the ground floor. I lost at least 2,000 photographs stored in my footlocker, photos of the Netherlands East Indies (now Indonesia) that I had planned to show my family back home in Indiana, photos of the native Filipino headhunters and the Moros, another native tribe. All my family pictures were gone too, along with the wristwatch my grandmother had given me when I was sixteen for not smoking.

When roll call was held in an apple orchard nearby,

we found that of nearly 200 men in our squadron, we had 14 known dead, 40 wounded and 6 missing.

Evening and the dreaded darkness it would bring were fast approaching and we had no place to sleep. The officers decided we would camp along the Margot River just past Stotsenburg, and they assembled us for the march there. We were ordered to disperse in groups a safe distance from one another yet close enough so that we could rush back to be together if Japanese paratroops started falling from the sky. We pitched two-man Army tents and dug new foxholes, just in case.

At this point I teamed up with Sergeant Paul Bellus, a guy from Tacoma, Washington. He proved to be a true comrade and a faithful buddy. I had seen him around Clark Field, but since he was our first sergeant's clerk and I was on a plane crew, our paths hadn't crossed much. Now we were tent buddies, and we dug a foxhole for mutual survival. The first night was spooky. We imagined that every little noise we heard, every little snap of a twig or rustle of a leaf was a Japanese paratrooper coming to kill us, or maybe a native headhunter brandishing his 6-foot-long spear.

The next morning we moved back to Clark Field to the old rifle butts that were built before World War I and now overrun by tall grass. Thick vegetation had camouflaged them so well we hadn't even known they existed. The rifle butts were long trenches dug in the ground, covered with a concrete slab and open on one side. Each trench was about 4 feet wide. One end of it was 6 feet high and it tapered to about 4 feet at the other end. Each man marked out a 7-foot spot to call home.

One of the soldiers, Private Mark, commandeered a

truck from Fort Stotsenburg and became a source of supplies for us. He rounded up cots and blankets, cans of food, clothes, and other such necessities. He was one of our favorite people. I accompanied him on a scavenging trip to Stotsenburg, to the bombed-out quartermaster building there. I helped myself to three pairs of khaki riding trousers, shirts, shorts, and a pair of high-top riding boots. The boots and riding pants would protect me from the snakes and insects I was bound to encounter in the heavy jungle growth.

General Douglas MacArthur (*right*) inspecting Bataan's defenses on October 10, 1941, with Major General Jonathan M. Wainwright.

Many Filipino civilians joined the evacuation of American troops, Filipino troops, and Filipino Scouts to the Bataan peninsula, just ahead of the advancing Japanese Army.

Refugees ready to leave Rosalea, Pangasinan 12-24-41

Chapter 10
MacArthur and Ike

"It is fatal to enter any war without the will to win it."
Douglas MacArthur in a 1952 speech to the Republican National Convention

Less than an hour after Hawaii was attacked on the December 7th, President Roosevelt established his strategic plan for running the war. He formed a group of high military, civilian, and diplomatic commanders. The group played right into Roosevelt's hands. No decision was made without his approval and the Roosevelt and Churchill "Europe First" initiative was born. Offensive action was to be waged against Germany and Italy first, then later against Japan.

General George C. Marshall selected Lieutenant Colonel Dwight D. Eisenhower, former deputy to MacArthur in the Philippines, to head Far East affairs for the military. Unfortunately, MacArthur and Eisenhower disliked each other.

According to Eisenhower in his book, *At Ease*, MacArthur and he had a fallout over plans for a parade while Eisenhower served under MacArthur in Manila before the outbreak of war. MacArthur thought that the morale of the Filipinos would be enhanced by a parade of their new Filipino Army in Manila. He entrusted Ike and another aide, James Ord, to make it happen. Ord and Ike reported back to MacArthur that there weren't funds available for the event, but were ordered to continue setting it up. After President Manuel Quezon and the Philippine government learned of the plans, they thought it too costly also and complained to MacArthur. Evidently, MacArthur denied to Quezon that he'd authorized Ord and Eisenhower to proceed with the parade plan, which caused considerable resentment.

Eisenhower's appointment as Head of the Far East desk by General Marshall wasn't a promising beginning for the relief of MacArthur and the Philippines.

The Philippines had been Pearl Harbor all over again. MacArthur's air strength was seriously crippled. Important questions remain unanswered to this day: Where was MacArthur during the early hours of the morning? Why was he hesitant to attack the Japanese on Formosa even though he had full knowledge of their attack on Pearl Harbor? Why were our planes caught on the ground, even after we reported that Japanese convoys were headed toward us? We had seen them with our own eyes. We had even photographed them!

Major General Brereton had received a blistering call from General Hap Arnold the night of December 8th demanding to know how in hell Brereton had been caught with all his planes at Clark neatly lined up to be destroyed after all the warnings. Numerous books were published by World War II leaders immediately after the end of the war. Brereton's was among the very first and it has been suggested by historians that his book was completed quickly to provide cover for his less than understandable actions.

However, whether intentional or not, Brereton's book does illustrate the defeatist attitude of some of our military leaders of the Philippines. An example was Admiral Thomas C. Hart's attitude. After Hart fled to Java with his Asiatic Fleet, he butted heads with Dutch Vice Admiral C. E. L. Helfrich. Helfrich wanted to use his Dutch fleet to fight the Japanese. According to Brereton, Hart continually argued against such bold tactics because the situation didn't call for such bold action. By this time, the American forces in the Philippines had fled to Bataan and Corregidor and Hart's fleet had fled south to Java and Australia. What would it have taken to light a fire under Hart, if this was true?

There's no doubt that Douglas MacArthur was caught by surprise when the Japanese planes swooped over Clark and Iba Fields, destroying half of his air force. At first, he even refused to believe that the pilots of those Japanese planes could have been Japanese nationals. He insisted that those pilots must have been white mercenaries.

MacArthur was hardly alone in believing the Japanese weren't capable of executing such an attack. The British in Hong Kong thought that Germans were leading the sorties over their airspace. Admiral Hart had dismissed the capability of the Dutch Navy in the East Indies because the Dutch ships had crews of mixed races. Former submariner Hart had some firm beliefs about the benefits of *apartheid* and was surprised that even the Dutch submarine crews were part Malay. The prejudices of these officers against the Japanese and other Asians contributed to the defeat of the U.S. and its Allies in the Far East.

On December 8, Roosevelt delivered his address to an

emergency session of Congress in Washington, D.C. "Yesterday, December 7, 1941—a date which will live in infamy—the United States was deliberately attacked by the naval and air forces of the emperor of Japan." Shortly afterward, he signed the declaration of war.

We heard that Winston Churchill's reaction to the Japanese invasion was, "so we won after all," meaning that now the United States would declare war on Japan and Germany. It pleased Churchill no end. That afternoon Roosevelt put his signature to the declaration of war against Japan. Churchill's declaration of war against Japan was actually two hours ahead of Roosevelt's. Both, however, were preceded by declarations of war by the Netherlands government-in-exile, the Netherlands East Indies, Canada, Costa Rica, and Nicaragua. They had all declared war on the Japanese the previous day.

This was the beginning of real British intervention and examination of the American military's resources and their use throughout World War II. The British used the personal magnetism of Winston Churchill to scrutinize the requirements of the Joint Chiefs of Staff. The British had their own ideas about the size and structure of American armed forces, the allocations of American food and oil, and American shipbuilding for the war.

In the Far East, the British demanded Allied support for their supposedly impregnable fortress at Singapore. It fell on February 15, 1942, after Allied resources had been wasted on its defense.

Queen Wilhelmina of the Netherlands explained why her nation was declaring war on the Japanese: "...because the aggression, that seeks to put out of action one by one the countries which desire peace, can only be halted through a strong coalition." This statement illustrates the beginning of Allied planning for a United Nations after the war.

Within three months, all Dutch forces in the East Indies would be obliterated by the Japanese.

The leaders of the Netherlands government-in-exile and the East Indies actually had something in common with the American soldiers, sailors, and airmen forced to retreat to Bataan and Corregidor in the Philippines: They all initially believed the American government's promises to send men and material to fight the Japanese aggression. But in reality, Marshall and Eisenhower were diverting planes, tanks and other war materials destined for the Far East to the war in Europe. Tanks paid for in advance by the Dutch for the East Indies were deliberately held back. Lend-Lease for the British meant easy credit and accessibility to American military supplies, thanks to the Roosevelt-Churchill connection. For the Dutch and others, Lend-Lease meant paying up front for weapons they might never receive.

(Top): Japanese crew members relaxed before taking off in their "Betty" bomber. The Japanese used the Betty to good advantage in their assault on the Philippines. *(Bottom)*: A Mitsubishi A6M3 fighter, commonly known as the "Zero." This clipped wing version was captured towards the end of World War II and displays American insignia.

Chapter II
Colin P. Kelly, Jr.

"We watched with horror as his B-17 was riddled with machine-gun fire."
Ralph M. Knox

Japanese planes continued to show up daily to bomb the Philippine Islands. They dropped bombs on Manila Bay, Del Carmen Field, Nichols and Nielson Fields, and Cavite Navy Base. They didn't forget Clark Field either. Some days they let us have it two or three times, interfering drastically with our urgent efforts to salvage parts from our damaged planes for shipment to Mindanao to be used in the planes there. All the B-17s we had left were on Mindanao at the Del Monte Pineapple Field. Those planes stayed in the air almost constantly to avoid being caught on the ground by the Japanese. During daylight hours, the pilots flew them in and around the island of Luzon and Manila, the capital city. From Mindanao, a few selected officers and personnel were flown to Australia.

On December 10, 1941, Captain Colin P. Kelly, Jr., was sent on an antishipping mission in one of the B-17Cs to bomb Japanese naval vessels and transport ships at Gonzaga. He was loaded with 500-pound bombs, but his plane had no rear gun turrets for self-protection.

None of our B-17Cs or B-17Ds had rear guns, and the Japanese made good use of that knowledge. Our pilots were able to compensate somewhat for this shortcoming by making quick, sudden turns when attacked from the rear. These maneuvers provided opportunities for the left and right waist gunners to shoot at Zeros approaching from behind.

On his return to Clark Field, Captain Kelly was intercepted by two Japanese Zeros and shot down in plain view of Clark's personnel. We watched with horror as his B-17 was riddled with machine gun fire. His crew bailed out, and the Japanese strafed their parachutes all the way to the ground. Captain Kelly went down with his B-17. He tried to bring in his shot-up plane for a belly landing, but missed the field by a 100 yards. His body was recovered later from the wreckage. More than 1,000 bullet holes were counted in the fuselage. Colin P. Kelly was our first war hero. He became the winner of the Distinguished Service Cross in the Philippines and was posthumously awarded the Medal of Honor for his heroism.

His surviving crew reported that Kelly had sunk the Japanese battleship *Haruna* on the mission, but later reports indicated that the *Haruna* was not in the area at the time. Most likely Kelly bombed the cruiser *Ashigari*, which did not sink.

On December 11, First Lieutenant Fischer, the first pilot I had flown with at Clark Field, and his two crewmen were lost at sea while ferrying a B-18 loaded with spare parts from Clark to Del Monte Field on Mindanao. No trace of them was ever found. We assumed the plane was overloaded and fell into the Pacific between Luzon and Mindanao. Fischer's wife had been with him at Clark Field but had returned to the States on one of the last evacuation ships prior to the war.

Three thousand Japanese troops landed at Legaspi, about 200 miles from Manila, the following day. We were on constant alert. Nurses tended the wounded and dying. Troops stood guard on tanks or on antiaircraft guns. We needed help badly, and we heard rumors that we'd get help soon. Convoys of men, equipment, and planes were supposedly on the way, and when they got there, we would be able to stop the onslaught of the Japanese. As time passed, however, it became apparent that nobody was coming. In fact, we noticed that more and more of our ranking officers were heading off to Australia. The bombing continued.

Before the initial attack on December 8th, we had been issued automatic .45-caliber pistols and gas masks. Now we were given helmets, shovels, mess kits, canteens, and rifles, either 1903 vintage rifles or World War I Enfields. The handwriting was on the wall. We couldn't defend Clark, so they were turning us into infantry soldiers. Shortly we'd be sent off to defend another part of the Philippines.

On December 12 and 13, more than 200 Japanese planes destroyed most of what was left of our Far East Air Force. Only 22 P-40s and six P-35s were in commission, along with the 16 B-17s hidden at Del Monte.

On December 16, the Japanese bombed Manila's docks, and on the 17th, General MacArthur ordered ten of Del Monte's B-17s to be flown to Batchelor Field near Darwin, Australia. The move was just in time because two days later the Japanese discovered our Del Monte hiding place.

MacArthur continually sent out messages requesting help. One read, "Please send me one P-40, as the one we have now is nearly worn out." That was our situation in a nut shell. We were helpless, yet the bombing continued and no help came. What little equipment we had was wearing out. A vote of no confidence in our leaders would have been in order.

The Japanese bombings kept on, as if on a schedule, and we flew our salvaged equipment and spare parts to Mindanao. We knew the Japanese army was getting closer as it moved through the mountains of Baguio. By December 24th, the Japanese were only one mile from Clark Field.

General Brereton left the Philippines on Christmas Eve. He closed his headquarters at Fort McKinley and flew off in a PBY to rejoin his bombers on Java. He was joined there by Colonel Eubank, who had been hit by a car during a blackout the previous week. Eubank suffered two sprained ankles, a broken wrist, and a cut on his head from the accident. Upon arrival on Java, Brereton himself required medical treatment. Brereton had foolishly handled some Japanese bomb fragments in an attempt to determine their weight and type. Both of his hands were treated by the USS *Houston*'s medical staff. Brereton and Eubank continued fighting the Japanese from Java until the situation there became untenable.

General Harold George, former Chief of Staff of the Interceptor Command, was in charge of the Far East Air Force for a short time. By the end of the month, 650 men of our 19th Bombardment Group had escaped to Java or Australia. They took with them any hope of our planes returning from Australia to help us. General George flew out of Del Monte field with MacArthur on March 17th.

Chapter 12
Bataan Bound

"If we really want to live,
we'd better start at once to try;
If we don't it doesn't matter,
we'd better start to die."
W. H. Auden, 1930

My group left the same day Brereton did, except we didn't go to Java or to Australia, we went to Bataan. Orders had come for all personnel on Clark Field and at Fort Stotsenburg to retreat to Bataan.

I'd never even heard of Bataan. But with the Japanese about a mile from Clark Field, I was happy to gather up my gear. I and my buddies loaded into the waiting buses and trucks. My tent buddy Bellus and I chose to ride topside on an old bus. Between us, we had what seemed a hoard of food—two cases of warm San Miguel beer, two tins of George Washington soda crackers, and five pounds of canned Spam.

Left behind was a huge supply of canned and frozen food, abandoned at Fort Stotsenburg to the Japanese by the poor planning of our military leaders. Later at Bataan and on Corregidor, we would desperately need those supplies.

As we pulled out of Clark, black clouds of smoke obliterated the landscape. We had purposely destroyed our remaining bomb dumps and fuel storage tanks. Off in the distance, we could hear the Japanese planes coming. Just outside the base, I spied a frightened baby goat by the side of the road and, cheered on by my topside companions, I climbed down off the bus and gently picked it up. Its shivering body gave no resistance. It seemed to welcome rescue.

Down the long, winding, dusty road to Bataan we rattled, amid hundreds of vehicles loaded down with soldiers and equipment. We expected the Japanese to attack us as we made our getaway, but they left us alone. Filipino civilians were evacuating too, and thousands of them crowded the road, on foot and in all sorts of rickety vehicles. They were fleeing from northern Luzon and Manila. Their thinking, of course, was that they would be safer with the American troops than being left behind in the hands of the Japanese.

After traveling all afternoon and evening of Christmas Eve, we finally arrived at the small village of Cabcaben near Mariveles on the lower tip of the Bataan peninsula. There we joined about 7,000 other American military personnel, all of whom were just as demoralized and disorganized as we were.

Our 28th bomb squadron chose a camp site off the road and about 100 yards from the coast. From there, we could see Corregidor, an island about the size of Manhattan three miles out in the Manila Bay. The heat and dust made caring for the pet goat difficult, so I let it go free.

The first order of business was to pitch tents, dig foxholes and dig straddle trenches for latrines. Bellus was busy putting together the company roster with the first sergeant, so I put up our two-man tent by myself. The crackers and Spam were long gone, and we were hungry again. The mess sergeant threw us some cans of corned beef and baked beans, not a very satisfying Christmas dinner.

Later we realized how bad off we really were. We lacked an adequate supply of mosquito nets, blankets, sun helmets, and quinine, a necessity for combating the malaria we would invariably contract. In our favor were a small stream nearby for cooling off and the huge trees in the mangrove forest that provided shade and shielded our camp from enemy planes.

During the first week we saw plenty of activity from the air. We witnessed the first bombing of Corregidor. Cavite, our naval base across the bay from us, was constantly being bombed. Black smoke billowed above it by day and fires lit up the base at night. At one point during that first week, a British merchant ship pulled up along our coastline, adjacent to our concealed camp. The freighter's Chinese crew quickly abandoned it, leaving the ship a wide-open target for the Japanese—and sitting right in our lap!

The Japanese air attack on December 10, 1941, on the Cavite Navy Yard, shown here, was similar to the bombings of the naval yard witnessed by Ralph M. Knox from his camp on the Bataan peninsula.

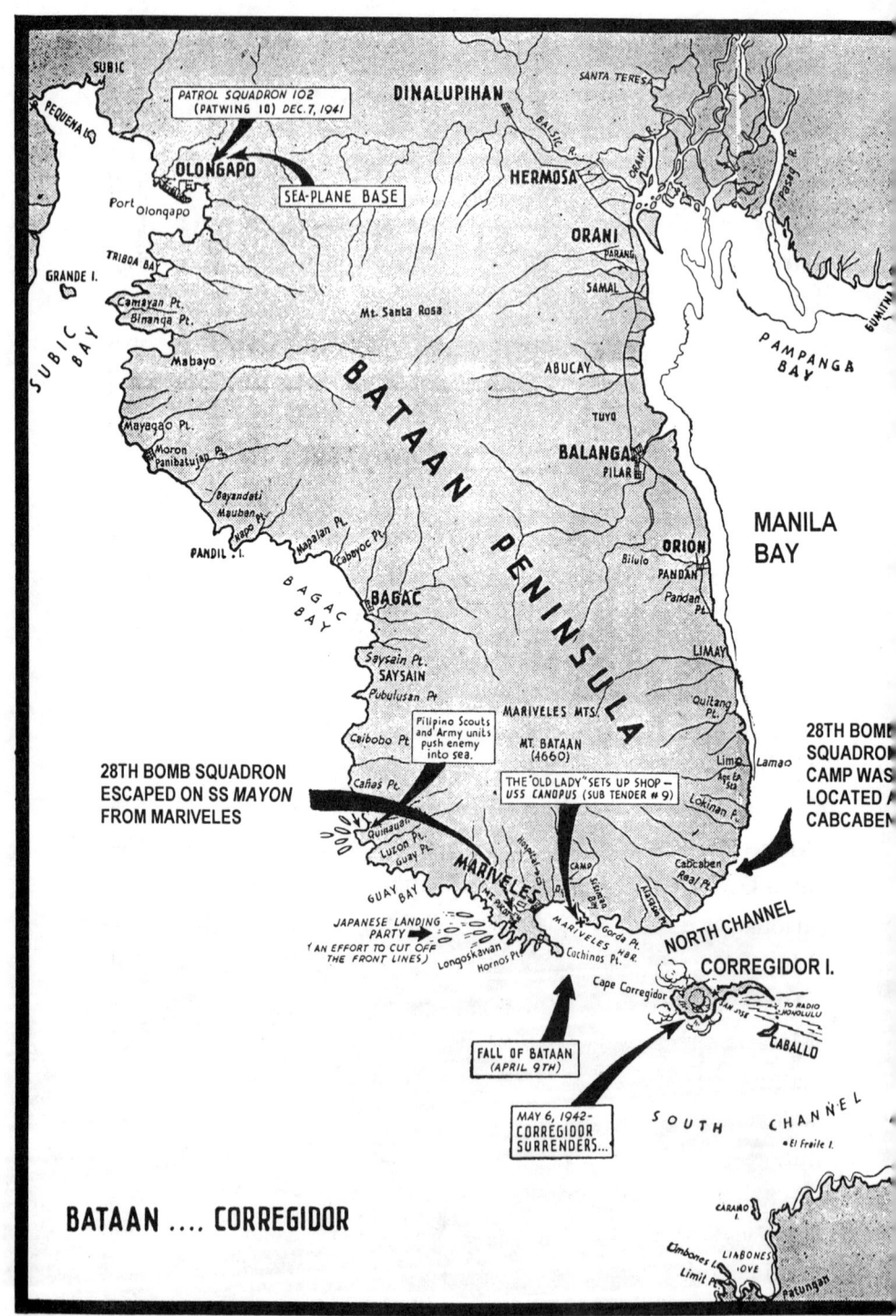

Ralph M. Knox's camp was located at Cabcaben at the southern end of the Bataan peninsula. He left Bataan on the SS *Mayon* from Mariveles.

Chapter 13
Smell of Defeat

> "...no spare parts for P-40s nor was there so much as an extra nut or washer for a Flying Fortress."
>
> Major General Lewis H. Brereton

There had been a running feud between General MacArthur and Admiral Hart in the Philippines for some time before December 8, 1941. Hart wanted to control all air operations launched against any Japanese invasion fleet at sea. MacArthur objected to using his Far East Air Force in support of Hart's fleet. In a November 7, 1941, letter to the admiral, MacArthur infuriated Hart by writing, "...the term 'Fleet' cannot be applied to two cruisers and the division of destroyers that comprise the surface elements of your command."

The uncooperative attitudes of the two highest military leaders in the Philippines influenced others down their chains of command. When the Army-Navy Club had to move 400 cases of whisky because Manila was being abandoned, the two services couldn't agree on jurisdiction. While the cases remained on a barge for four days, the army and navy argued until a Japanese bomb ended the argument and the whisky on the fourth day.

The disagreements between the services in the Philippines stemmed in part from divided authority. The army and its air force were supposedly responsible for defending America's overseas possessions, but the navy was responsible for the patrol duty required to alert the army defenders.

We had heard that Wake Island had fallen on December 23rd and that 120 Americans and 800 Japanese died in the battle for the island. A combination of 1,500 Americans, both military and civilian, surrendered on Wake. Rumor then had it that Hong Kong fell on Christmas Day.

These losses were quickly put on the back burner by the news that Churchill was staying at the White House with Roosevelt and the two were plotting their roles in the war against Germany. *The Philippines Herald* headlined an article on its December 25, 1941, front page: "U.S.-British Confab Said Progressing." The Reuters article under the headline continued: "At a joint press conference earlier yesterday, the premier and the president described how Britain and the United States, with other nations opposing the Axis, expect to wipe out Hitlerism from the face of the earth." There was no mention of help for American and Allied forces in the Far East.

Churchill was ensconced on the second floor of the White House within two weeks of Pearl Harbor, using it as a communication center and a plotting room. In Roosevelt's meetings with Churchill, the president agreed that Germany's defeat would take priority over the war with Japan.

Americans on the home front admired Churchill. They felt uplifted by his tenacity, his courage and his confidence. His mother was Jennie Jerome, a New Yorker. American admiration was mixed with pride that he was half American and half English. One commentator wasn't fooled, though. He said Churchill was "half American and ALL English."

Undoubtedly that's why, and when, the decision was made, to divert to Australia any reinforcements headed for the Philippines. That's also why American soldiers received no assistance in the Philippines.

On December 23, MacArthur regained his fourth star, and facing the inevitable that he could not save the Philippines, he urgently requested fighter aircraft. It was the next day that MacArthur fully realized that the half-trained, ill-equipped Filipino troops were weak and not capable of stopping the hard-core, seasoned Japanese warriors. Even General Jonathan Wainwright, who led the Filipino troops, described them as a mob.

All troop reinforcements and aircraft convoys en route to Manila were diverted to Australia by General Marshall. After Brereton ordered the B-17s from the Philippines to Port Darwin, both Marshall and Secretary of War Stimson put the question to Eisenhower, the newly-assigned director of war plans, "Should we or not give up the Philippines?" Eisenhower, who suffered under MacArthur's command three years earlier in Manila, did not provide his approval to aid and defend the Philippines.

This Japanese photograph shows one of the signs hung over the streets that declared Manila an open city on December 26, 1941.

Chapter 14
Manila Envelope

"The bloodied envelope addressed to you,
Is history, that wide and mortal pang."
                        Stanley Kunitz, from *Night Letter*

MacArthur sealed Manila's fate by declaring it an "open city," an old tactic of war that was supposed to spare the city further violence. *The Philippines Herald* on Christmas Day asked in an editorial: "What guarantees are there that the safety of an open city will be respected by the enemy?"

Evidently, not many. In spite of the city being declared as such on December 26th, the Japanese were still bombing it in great earnest as late as December 27. We saw it happening from our tent site.

MacArthur hadn't consulted the head of our Asiatic Fleet, Admiral Hart, before declaring Manila an open city. Hart was furious because the navy was still using the Cavite Naval Base there. When told by a subordinate about the declaration of the open city, Hart jumped up and yelled, "What!

Come around here and sit down and write that down." Then Hart stared at the piece of paper, fuming.

Perhaps the Japanese continued their bombings over Manila on December 26 and 27 because the navy was still active on the docks.

Days on Bataan were long, disrupted only by waves of Japanese bombers flying directly over our camp on their way to unload on Corregidor. It was sad to watch. The Japanese flew at about 29,000 feet, but Corregidor's antiaircraft guns could reach only 27,000 feet at the most. We had heard that MacArthur and his family had retreated to Corregidor, and when bombardments became intolerable, they moved into the island's hundred-foot-long Malinta Tunnel.

On December 28, Corregidor was hit hard at noon by 18 Japanese bombers escorted by 19 fighters. Half an hour later a second wave of 22 light bombers and 19 dive bombers hit Corregidor, followed by a third wave of Japanese Navy fighters. More than half the wooden buildings on the island were destroyed.

That night Bellus and I walked to a small village outside our camp. Crowds of Filipino civilians mingled in the balmy night air. We could sense their anxiety and see the cold fear in their faces. I struck up a conversation with a beautiful young Filipino girl named Primitiva Gaboli and her family. They offered to help me escape. In exchange for my .45-caliber pistol, they would provide me with a small native boat, in which, they suggested, I could make my way to Corregidor or some other island south of Luzon. I did not take them up on their offer.

After having a few beers at a shack temporarily turned

into a bar, Bellus and I returned to our tent feeling mighty low. Rumors were flying high that two of our three squadrons would be going to Australia. I wanted to be in that group.

The following morning, the representative of our Air Force group called us together and confirmed the rumors. At least one squad would go to Australia. The others would stay to defend Bataan. Besides my outfit, the 28th Bomb Group, there were the 14th and 30th Bomb Groups. The idea of staying behind made us all nervous. It seemed sure death.

I wanted desperately to go to Australia. I was not a rifleman, I was an airman. I didn't know how to fight like an infantryman. Two wildly different pictures unfolded in my mind, one of me and a crew in a shiny, new plane flying in triumphantly like the cavalry in a western movie to free our comrades; the other was of dark days suffering humiliating defeat, torture, and death.

Major M. F. Daly decided to flip a coin to decide who went and who stayed. When it came time for my group's toss, I said a silent prayer. It worked. My squadron was going to Australia! I didn't know which to do, cry or leap up and down shouting with joy. After seeing the dejected faces of the losers, however, I knew self-control was the better choice. To show too much happiness would have been exceedingly cruel. I learned later that the 14th Bomb Squadron didn't stay on Bataan but had been moved to Mindanao.

The goers and the stayers gathered around one another, hugging, shaking hands, slapping each others' backs, promising to contact families and sweethearts for friends when we reached Australia. Those bound for Australia gave all their food, cigarettes, clothes, toiletries, and ammunition to the men who would stay behind on Bataan.

My last night on Bataan was December 30, 1941. I returned to the little village to find Primitiva, the young woman I had met the night before. I liked her and wanted to see her again before I left. Confused civilians and military personnel clustered around the village, slowing my progress, but I finally located Primitiva sitting with her parents on a wooden bench. She was as happy to see me as I was to see her. For most of the night, we held hands and strolled around. If I hadn't wanted to go to Australia so badly, I might have chosen to stay with her.

This barbed wire was part of the beach defenses along the shores of Bataan peninsula.

Chapter 15
SS *Mayon* to Mindanao

> "Carmen Ferry wasn't nearly as attractive as Carmen Miranda."
> Ralph M. Knox

The next morning, 300 lucky men climbed aboard the inter-island steamer, the SS *Mayon*. We were on our way. We carried only a bedroll, a pistol, and a few rounds of ammunition. Before we moved away from the pier, a Japanese plane came in over the Bay of Manila and dropped two bombs on us. One hit the rear edge of the ship's fantail; the other missed, but not by much.

Panic broke out. A few soldiers jumped into the bay. Others yelled for us all to hit the deck and lay flat. The plane turned to make another pass. The *Mayon*'s captain ordered a quick maneuver in the boiler room that caused the smoke stacks to spit out a huge stream of black smoke. It spread over the ship like a blanket. The bombs on the second pass fell far from the ship, but the concussion from the bombs seriously injured the men who had jumped into the water. At least two were killed.

The enemy plane disappeared. He either ran out of bombs or thought he had sunk the ship. Soon after, we got under way, heading south through mine fields in Manila Bay and into the South China Sea. The intent had been to sail under the protection of darkness, but since we'd already been sighted, we decided to get the hell out. It was New Year's Eve. The following morning we anchored somewhere off the southern tip of the island of Mindoro.

During the night of January 1, 1942, we traveled another 200 miles or so, pulling in under cover off Negros Island. Crowded into the steamer like cattle, the men began to get restless. No beds were available, so when we wanted to catch some shut-eye, we just unrolled our blankets wherever we were. I heard years later that a columnist in the states had dubbed 1942 "Nineteen-Fortitude." That certainly was an apt description of the beginning of the new year for us.

The SS *Mayon* kept up its steam but not much speed. Plans were made to stop at Mindanao, where the captain hoped to have some needed repairs made to the ship. We moved along mostly at night. Once, off on the horizon, we spotted a submarine. It could have been either Japanese or American, but it didn't spot us.

On the second day of the new year, we disembarked at Bugo, on Mindanao Island.

The SS *Mayon* turned out to be in bad shape and Mindanao lacked the facilities to make needed repairs, so the ship and crew headed back north toward Mariveles or Corregidor. The *Mayon* was attacked and sunk on the way back.

The next morning we were ordered to go across Mindanao, on the only highway available, to a river and camp at Carmen Ferry.

Our convoy consisted of two GI trucks: one loaded with a field kitchen and supplies; the other one was loaded with our food, flour, rice, sugar, and C-rations. We had very few canned goods. There were four buses to transport the 65 enlisted men and 15 officers that remained with our outfit.

Our total armament was five .30-caliber machine guns, and either a rifle or .45 pistol for each man. Each man had about 80 rounds of ammunition.

The "highway" was a dirt road and, because it was the rainy season, it seemed we spent most of our time pushing the vehicles through thick mud instead of riding in them.

Log bridges across the flooded streams had washed out, too, and we had to rebuild them to get across. The mountainside was unbelievably steep. One wrong move, and our trucks or buses would have hurtled several thousand feet straight down.

By that night though, we were in Malaybalay, the capital, in the center of Mindanao. Everything was in total blackout. The command post for the Davao-Digos front, under Brigadier General Joseph P. Vachon, was located here.

A Moro chieftain named Piang met us when we were only 50 kilometers or so from Carmen Ferry. Somehow, he knew we were coming and welcomed us with homemade cigars, which he distributed as gifts. He and his men escorted us the rest of the way. We immediately designated him an honorary captain.

Carmen Ferry was a village of six buildings. We set up camp there and placed machine guns along the river bank so we could defend ourselves if the Japanese chose to try a river crossing. We were divided into four platoons and each group was responsible for a machine gun or two. Meanwhile we listened to the radio messages to and from the Davao-Digos front, which was not far away.

I began to get weary. What was going to happen next? Everything seemed to be going wrong. Even our tents at Carmen Ferry had been washed away during the night in a torrential rain, so common in the islands at this time of year. I longed for the flat farmland of Indiana, perhaps covered now with a crisp winter snow. I chastised myself, for about the thousandth time, for ever joining up in this damned army.

To keep my sanity, I kept myself busy. I became a runner for the 28th squadron. In our spare time, my buddies and I explored nearby caves. They were unbelievable. We had underground caves in Indiana, but nothing like this. Most of the caves on Mindanao had ledges lining the inside walls and on those ledges, which were about eye level, lounged pythons 25 to 30 feet long. The snakes weren't dangerous. They were just resting there, letting their meal digest. Pythons kill their prey, usually a pig or a deer, by squeezing it to death, then swallowing it whole. Afterward, they just loll around while the whole thing digests. Bats lived in the caves too, big ones with wingspans nearly 5 feet across. It's too bad we didn't have a camera to record our adventures into those caves.

I could have used a camera on another occasion too. Sergeant Bellus and I attended a private Moro ceremony. It took place in a clearing in the jungle. Wearing native finery and feathers, the Moros chanted, danced, and cooked a feast for us over a barbecue-like pit. Each man wore a ceremonial kris, which was a large dagger with a wavy blade. The

Moros kept time on drums crafted from hollowed-out logs covered with animal skins. Bellus and I had no idea what was happening, but it was an unforgettable experience anyway.

Bathroom facilities were sorely lacking, so we bathed in the river at Carmen Ferry. We were constantly on the lookout for the 18-foot crocodiles that inhabited the river. When we emerged from the water, we always examined each other for the leeches that lived in the river and invariably attached themselves to our skin. We never failed to find the slimy blood-suckers clinging somewhere on our body, often in an unmentionable place. The leeches were four or five inches long and you couldn't pull them off. The only way to get the leeches to turn loose was to stick the hot end of a cigarette to them, then they fell right off.

Our latrines, or straddle trenches as we called them, were a source of entertainment at times too. We dug long, narrow trenches for toilets. When nature called, we straddled over the opening, but never at night because snakes, including deadly king cobras, would invariable crawl in and not be able to crawl out. For fun, we paid Filipino native boys to reach into the trench, grab a cobra, and kill it. For two pesos, the boys would put on quite a show. First, they would reach a hand out over the trench and move it very slowly toward the snake, then grab the snake by the neck and whack its head off with a bolo held in the other hand. The natives, young and old, were experts with bolos, their sharp machete-like knives.

During the early part of March, Brigadier General William F. Sharp, the American commander on Mindanao, called for two volunteers to deliver .50 caliber machine-gun ammunition to the Digos front on the Davao Gulf. Corporal Robert J. Endrees and I volunteered for the assignment. We were driven by truck to General Sharp's headquarters somewhere close to Malaybalay. The general towered over his staff; his height surprised me. He talked to Endrees and me for at least an hour, asking about our service and when we first arrived in the Philippines and bits about our families back in the States. Then he led us to a four-door 1938 LaSalle already loaded and ready to go. Ammo filled the trunk and the interior where the back seat had been. He told us to follow highway 3 south to the intersection of highway 1, then southeast to a hemp plantation outside of Bansalan for the drop off.

The 160-mile trip down narrow, winding, mountainous gravel roads took us two days. The first day out, a Japanese plane spotted us and made several attempts to strafe us, but the twisting, hilly road saved us. Every time the plane lined us up for the kill, we rounded a hill. Finally he got tired of playing cat and mouse and left. Endrees and I had been so scared we forgot we were in a portable bomb carrier.

Because snipers might spot us, we dared not drive in the dark, so the first night we pulled the LaSalle over to the side of the road to sleep. The evening air was stiflingly hot, so we left the windows rolled down. Shortly, we heard rustling in the weeds just outside our car. We were petrified. We thought the Japanese had found us for sure. Just as we were ready to stick our hands up to surrender, a water buffalo stuck its head in the window. Neither of us slept for the rest of the night, and as soon as it began to get light, we went on our way.

No Americans met us at the hemp plantation. We turned the ammunition over to the Filipino troops, turned around and drove home. General Sharp congratulated us on a successful journey and asked us how we liked being chased down by a Japanese plane. One of his guerrilla operators out in the field had reported our encounter with the Japanese to him by radio. For being part of the mission, General Sharp promoted me from Sergeant to Staff Sergeant and Endrees from Corporal to Sergeant. The general also promised he would recommend both of us for a Silver Star.

I later learned that Sergeant Endrees did indeed get his Silver Star, but I never got mine.

General Sharp was ill-equipped to fight a war and he admitted it. He said his men could better outlast the Japanese as guerrilla fighters until and if help came. He was short of blankets, uniforms, mosquito nets. His Filipino soldiers were equipped with 1917 Enfield rifles, no antitank guns, no grenades, no gas masks, no steel helmets, and no artillery weapons, and of course he couldn't count on air or naval support. It was lunacy to think that we were in a war under those pitiful conditions.

Major General William F. Sharp, front row, fourth from the left, and his staff in early 1942, somewhere near Malaybalay on Mindanao.

Chapter 16
Doug Departs

> "I'm going to the latrine, but I shall return."
>
> Popular satire among the troops left behind in the Philippines after they heard about MacArthur's "I shall return" speech in Australia

As early as February of 1942, there was little hope in Washington, D.C., or in the Philippines, that the American and Filipino troops could withstand the Japanese forces for more than a few months.

On February 8, Manuel Quezon, the president of the Philippines, wanting to save his nation from further disaster, sent a message to President Roosevelt proposing that the United States grant the Philippines their independence, neutralize the islands, and withdraw by mutual agreement all American and Japanese forces. In his message, Quezon stated clearly his disillusion with the government of the United States. After nine weeks of fighting, he pointed out, not even a small amount of aid had reached the Philippines from the United States. Instead, the U.S. had sent help and assistance to other, belligerent, nations.

General MacArthur, in his own message to Washington, haphazardly approved Quezon's proposal. The War Department was shocked and perhaps for the first time recognized that the battle in the Philippines was a lost cause.

Washington's reaction was quick and direct: No! On February 9, in a message drafted by Secretary of War Henry L. Stimson, Roosevelt pledged continued American support, stating that as long as the American flag flew on Philippine soil, it would be defended by Americans to the death. Roosevelt then sent a message to MacArthur advising that he could surrender the Philippine troops, if necessary, but he forbade the surrender of American troops.

On February 15, Singapore, Britain's stronghold in the Far East, fell. Already Malaya, Borneo, and the Celebes had fallen. On that same day, the U.S. and Britain turned over command for the defense of the East Indies to the Dutch. Roosevelt and Churchill had decided it was best to let the Dutch take the rap for the coming defeat there. America's Admiral Thomas C. Hart, after turning over his command to Dutch Vice Admiral C. E. L. Helfrich, left the East Indies in civilian clothes.

Admiral Hart and General MacArthur had been the top commanders of the U.S. Navy and Army in the Philippines. They had not conferred since December 1941, and they would never meet one another again.

February 15, 1942 was a very lucrative day for General MacArthur, his Chief of Staff Richard Sutherland and two other officers on MacArthur's staff. Though serving officers in the U. S. Army were expressly forbidden to accept what might be called "golden handshakes" today, $500,000 was transferred from the Philippine Treasury to a private account in New York belonging to General MacArthur. Another $140,000 was transferred out of the Philippine Treasury to benefit Sutherland and the other two officers. President Quezon had authorized these payments in January 1942 as "recompense and reward, however inadequate, for distinquished service." It was a good thing for MacArthur and the other officers that American and Filipino soldiers on Bataan and Corregidor didn't know about these "rewards."

Roosevelt ordered MacArthur to Australia, but left the day and time of departure up to the general himself. At first MacArthur refused to leave. Eventually, he chose March 16, the ides of March, for his escape from the Philippines. Arrangements for the trip were made by Rear Admiral Francis Rockwell, the naval commander left on Corregidor, and MacArthur's aide, General Richard Sutherland.

MacArthur promised there was enough food and ammunition on Bataan to last through June, enabling the defenders of Bataan to hold out until his expected return on July 1.

On March 12, four PT boats carrying MacArthur's party of twenty-one sailed from Corregidor under cover of darkness on the first leg of their journey. Lieutenant John D. Bulkeley led the convoy and commanded PT-41, MacArthur's boat. Traveling in it with him were the general's wife, their son Arthur, the boy's Chinese amah, an army doctor, and the general's aides. Also aboard was "General Tojo," the cook's monkey. Little Arthur played with the monkey, which pretty much had the run of the ship. Lieutenant Robert B. Kelly commanded PT-34, Ensign Anthony Akers commanded PT-35 and Lieutenant (jg) V. S. Schumacher commanded PT-

32. MacArthur's plan was to travel to Del Monte Field on Mindanao, the southernmost Philippine island, then leave the Philippines by plane on March 16.

After sailing throughout the first night, the boats landed on a small uninhabited island in the Cuyo Islands. During the night, one of the PT boats had become separated, and PT-32 ran out of fuel because it had dumped its spare fuel when it mistook another of the PTs for the enemy. The passengers of that boat were taken aboard the others, and the group continued south. The remaining three PT boats reached Mindanao the morning of March 14, 1942.

Brigadier General William F. Sharp, the American commander on Mindanao, met the group and took them to Del Monte Airfield, where 17 of Colonel Eubank's original 35 B-17s had been sent in November. All of our planes were long since gone, but four B-17s had been requisitioned from Australia. Of the four, only one actually arrived, on March 11th, and it was in bad shape. Two had turned back and one had crashed.

MacArthur's group stayed on Mindanao for three days, awaiting decent planes to fly them to Australia. Three more B-17s were dispatched from Australia.

Weeks before, several other mechanics and I were sent to Del Monte Airfield, and when we arrived, the place looked like a graveyard. Only one complete B-17 was there, and it didn't look like it could fly. Crates loaded with spare plane parts, some of the very ones I had packed up on Clark Field months ago, were scattered everywhere. We salvaged and repaired the B-18s and B-17s at Del Monte and repacked the spare parts and sent them off to Australia.

It was rumored that four B-17s were coming in from Darwin, Australia, and one did arrive on March 11. It was in such bad shape, however, that it looked and its sputtering sounded as if it would never take off again. Of the four B-17s that had set out from Australia, one had crashed into the ocean off Mindanao's coast and two had turned back midway.

Around midnight on March 16, two more B-17s arrived, part of the latest group of three B-17s dispatched from Australia. They were B-17E's with the larger tail, and looked decent.

Later that night General Sharp led a large convoy onto the airfield. It didn't take us long to realize that it was General Douglas MacArthur, himself, with his wife Jean, their 4-year-old son Arthur, and the boy's Chinese amah, Au Cheu. They were accompanied by more military top brass than I had ever seen assembled in one place:

> Gen. Richard K. Sutherland, Chief of Staff
> Capt. Harold G. Ray, U.S. Navy
> Lt. Col. Sidney L. Huff, Aide
> Maj. Charles H. Morhouse, Medical Officer
> Adm. Francis W. Rockwell, U.S. Navy
> Gen. Richard J. Marshall, Sutherland's deputy
> Col. Charles P. Stivers, G-1
> Capt. Joseph McMicking, (PA) Asst. G-2
> Col. Charles A. Willoughby, G-2
> Lt. Col. LeGrand A. Diller, Aide
> Lt. Col. Francis H. Wilson, Aide to Sutherland
> M. Sgt. Paul P. Rogers, Secretary
> Brig. Gen. Spencer B. Akin, Signal Corps
> Brig. Gen. Hugh J. Casey, Engineer Chief

Brig. Gen. William F. Marquat, AA. Officer
Brig. Gen. Harold H. George, Air Officer
Lt. Col. Joe R. Sherr, Asst. Sig. Officer

The airmen and other personnel at Del Monte were totally astonished to meet and be able to talk to the officers in this distinguished group. Now we knew why the original four B-17s were ordered up from Australia! MacArthur's group must have been exasperated to find only one crippled B-17 awaiting them on Mindanao when they first arrived.

Using parts from a B-17 that had previously crashed at the field and from the depleted supply of parts available, we were able to put the crippled B-17 that had landed March 11th back in service. Now considered airworthy, we were ordered to load it with the personal belongings of General MacArthur, his family, and the other 18 people in his party. We filled that plane with footlockers, crates of clothing and fur coats, pipe tobacco, several straight back chairs, little Arthur MacArthur's toys, one rocking chair and two particularly heavy mattresses.

As we were loading the mattresses, someone said, "There goes the Philippine gold." Actually, the gold and silver of the Philippines were taken out in an American submarine, the USS *Trout*. As American sailors loaded the rotted bags of silver coins taken from Manila's vaults onto the *Trout*, many of the bags ripped apart, spilling much of the treasure into Manila Bay.

More than one of the airmen loading that B-17 bomber remarked that American nurses should have been evacuated on the plane, instead of footlockers loaded with personal effects. Why didn't MacArthur take an American nurse with him to look after his son instead of the Chinese amah? General

George Marshall actually asked that question when he learned that MacArthur brought his Chinese amah out.

William Manchester, in his biography of MacArthur, *American Caesar*, reported that only one mattress was loaded on any of the planes and that there were only two B-17s. According to Manchester, Lieutenant Colonel Sidney Huff personally loaded the one mattress, and it was for little Arthur. But I was there, and I didn't see any officer load anything onto any plane. Most important of all, there were three B-17s that took off for Australia that night. None of the versions written by historians about MacArthur and his party fleeing the Philippines mentions the third B-17.

Little Arthur cried constantly while at the airfield. After the war I learned he had been ill on the PT-boat trip from Corregidor to Australia, which would certainly account for his nonstop wailing.

MacArthur's entire entourage was squeezed aboard the two B-17Es that arrived on March 16. Everyone in his party graciously accepted our notes or letters for loved ones with promises they would see to it that those letters were forwarded to our families in the States.

The B-17 carrying MacArthur's worldly goods was the first to take off. About 20 minutes later, shortly after midnight on March 17th, the two B-17Es carrying the passengers, lined up and took off. They disappeared in the sky, heading south.

I still get emotional and misty-eyed whenever I think about them departing, leaving us behind, knowing full well our expected fate. The airfield seemed so empty and lonely after the three planes disappeared over the horizon. Obviously, my buddies and I would not be completing our own trip to Australia. MacArthur's soldiers, both American and

Filipino, stayed behind to be sacrificed. We had become cannon fodder.

I can't help wondering even now why MacArthur and his party didn't deem it more important to evacuate Americans instead of luggage and toys? Especially now that I know that MacArthur and Sunderland had fortunes waiting for them back in New York, courtesy of President Quezon.

After the war, I asked my mother if indeed she had received the letter I had hastily written on the runway at Del Monte Field in 1942 and placed in the hands of MacArthur's group. She never had.

Many bitter poems about Dugout Doug's escape to Australia were written and passed around by the enlisted men and junior officers of Bataan. One ditty went like this:

> In Australia's fresh clime,
> he took out the time
> to send us a message of cheer.
> "My heart," he began,
> "Goes out to Bataan,
> But the rest of me's
> Staying right here."

Lieutenant Bulkeley later received the Medal of Honor "For extraordinary heroism, distinguished service, and conspicuous gallantry above and beyond the call of duty as commander of Motor Torpedo Boat Squadron 3, in Philippine waters during the period 7 December 1941 to 10 April 1942."

Bulkeley himself was described as a "wild man" by many of those who knew him at that time. He resembled a swashbuckling pirate, with his long, unkempt beard and two pistols. Because of his constant night patrols among the Philippine Islands, his eyes were always bloodshot.

After landing MacArthur on Mindanao, Lieutenants Bulkeley and Kelly, in PT-41 and PT-35, attacked and probably sank a Japanese warship near Cebu Island. Kelly's boat was bombed and strafed by the Japanese the next day. The boat was beached and three of its crew were either killed or wounded.

The PT officers themselves finally arrived in Australia in late April 1942. Lieutenant Bulkeley and Ensign Akers arrived first. Lieutenant Kelly arrived later. Lieutenant Schumacher had arrived by submarine in March after his PT-32 had to be scuttled.

When MacArthur left the Philippines, he said, "I shall return," but what the general failed to say was *when*. To be fair, he probably had every intention of returning by July. He planned to assemble enough troops, warships, planes, and supplies to make an early and decisive return to Bataan and Corregidor. But when MacArthur arrived in Australia, he found disarray, lack of leadership, and very few supplies or troops to launch an effective campaign. There were only 25,000 American troops in Australia, and they were mostly airmen and engineers. He had no riflemen, no tanks, no artillery, and only a few decrepit combat aircraft. Eisenhower had seen to it that the Australian cupboard was bare.

If MacArthur had been able to send help back to the Philippines as he had promised, the Japanese might have been prevented from consolidating their footholds on the many islands along the Malay Archipelago and in the Pacific. The ability of the Japanese to support and supply their many troops in their newly acquired, far-flung empire might have been made more difficult.

There's no doubt sending help would have been a huge

undertaking. The Netherlands East Indies, spreading across a 3,000-mile-wide island chain from Sumatra to New Guinea, and separating the Philippines from Australia, officially surrendered on March 8. The Japanese had defeated the Allied fleet in the Java Sea on February 27 through March 1. The Allies lost five destroyers and five cruisers, including the heavy cruiser USS *Houston*, the only modern surface vessel stationed in the Philippines as part of the U.S. Asiatic Fleet. Roosevelt had cruised on the *Houston* in the 1930s. Whatever Allied ships and planes we had left were fleeing south ahead of MacArthur.

One Dutch mine sweeper, the *Abraham Crijnssen*, fled south to Australia disguised as a small island.

A PT boat roars through Philippine waters. Four similar PT boats carried General Douglas MacArthur and his party as they made their escape from Corregidor to Mindanao.

Chapter 17
King Surrenders Bataan

> "—And nobody gives a damn."
> The defenders of Bataan

After MacArthur's retreat to Australia, confusion reigned among military commanders over control of the troops abandoned in the Philippines. MacArthur decided that he would continue controlling all forces in the Philippines and that he would do so from Australia. MacArthur divided the Philippines into four subcommands. Major General Jonathan "Skinny" Wainwright would control the Luzon forces; General George Moore would command Corregidor; Brigadier General William F. Sharp would command the entire southern island of Mindanao; and Brigadier General Bradford G. Chynoweth would command the Visayans, the islands in the center.

Unfortunately, MacArthur forgot to tell his bosses in Washington about his new organization of command. They assumed in Washington that Wainwright, as the ranking officer, was MacArthur's replacement and, thus, the supreme commander of the Philippines.

No one left behind in the Philippines knew what was going on. Even President Roosevelt's messages were addressed to Wainwright, and the War Department ordered Wainwright to send daily reports. When MacArthur heard about the mix-up, he explained to the War Department the structure he had left behind. Roosevelt, however, didn't favor the plan, stating that it seemed impossible for MacArthur to run a war on Luzon by radio from Australia.

Roosevelt promoted Wainwright to Lieutenant General and left Wainwright under MacArthur's command but gave him autonomy on running the war in the Philippines. The U.S. Forces in the Philippines (USFIP) command was created and Wainwright was appointed its commander. MacArthur accepted it.

Wainwright moved his command to Corregidor. He appointed Major General Edward P. King, Jr., as commander of all Luzon forces, which were mostly on Bataan.

Food on Bataan was in extremely short supply. Men were on less than 1,000 calories a day. They had depleted the jungle of anything edible, and, as usual, promises of food supplies had not been fulfilled. Malnutrition combined with malaria and dysentery took its toll, and the Japanese kept coming.

The food shortage was mainly MacArthur's fault. Food had been stored in Luzon in large dumps, but MacArthur never transported enough of it to where it would do the most good. Bataan, for example.

Hundreds of tons of food were stored at Fort

Stotsenburg. But when the Americans abandoned the fort, perhaps prematurely, the food was left behind. Cabanatuan had a huge Philippine rice dump, but the Philippine government had a regulation that rice could not be moved from one province to the other.

Filipino workers abandoned the railroads and there were no crews to operate the trains. The Philippine government would not allow American troops to take over the trains, so tons of food were not moved to Bataan.

Japanese food exporters in the Philippines, with warehouses loaded with canned fish and corned beef, were not taken over by the U.S. and the contents of their warehouses were not confiscated. MacArthur's headquarters would not allow an American colonel to take over the Japanese owned warehouses.

By early April 1942, Bataan's days were numbered. General King's 80,000 Filipino and American troops were starving and diseased. Many Filipino soldiers had thrown down their weapons and gone home.

On Corregidor, Wainwright was aware of King's situation, and he informed both Marshall in Washington and MacArthur in Australia. General Funk, King's Chief of Staff, went to Australia to advise MacArthur of the impending surrender. MacArthur sent a message to Wainwright that he was not to surrender under any circumstances. He maintained that directive even after Wainwright made it clear that, if food did not arrive, the troops on Bataan would starve. Roosevelt's message of "no surrender" complicated the situation. Under ludicrous orders from both Roosevelt and MacArthur, Wainwright advised General Funk that Bataan must be held. He even ordered General King to counterattack.

But the night of April 8, King advised Wainwright that if he expected to move any troops to Corregidor, he would have to do it that night, as it would be too late after that. King made the decision to surrender Bataan on his own. He stated that he could no longer sacrifice more lives.

Colonel E.C. Williams and Major Marshall H. Hurt volunteered to carry the white flag of surrender to Japan's front lines. During the night, all munitions and such supplies were destroyed. Nurses from two field hospitals were evacuated to Corregidor. At daylight, Williams and Hurt reached the Japanese front and were taken to meet General Nagano. Nagano agreed to meet King at Lamao, near the front line. When Wainwright learned of King's surrender, he was still opposed to it.

At about 9 a.m. on April 9, King was on his way to meet Nagano. Though confusion ensued, King finally made it clear that he was surrendering Bataan only and requested that his men be treated under the guidelines of the Geneva Convention. The Japanese, however, insisted that all forces in the Philippines be included in the surrender, and until there was a total surrender, they would treat the Bataan forces as hostages, not as prisoners of war.

The Voice of Freedom broadcast the following message from Corregidor announcing the fall of Bataan. It was written by Salvador Lopez and read by Norman Reyes.

Bataan has fallen. The Philippine-American troops on this war-ravaged and blood-stained peninsula have laid down their arms. With heads bloody but unbowed, they have yielded to the superior force and numbers of the enemy....

The world will long remember the epic struggle that Filipino and American soldiers put up in these jungle fastnesses and along the rugged coast of Bataan. They have stood uncomplaining under the constant and grueling fire of the enemy for more than three months. Besieged on land and blockaded by sea, cut off from all sources of help in the Philippines and in America, these intrepid fighters have done all that human endurance could bear.

For what sustained them through all these months of incessant battle was a force that was more than merely physical. It was the force of an unconquerable faith—something in the heart and soul that physical hardship and adversity could not destroy! It was the thought of native land and all that it holds most dear, the thought of freedom and dignity, the pride in these most priceless of all human prerogatives.

The adversary, in the pride of his power and triumph, will credit our troops with nothing less than the courage and fortitude that his own troops have shown. All the world will testify to the almost superhuman endurance with which they stood up until the last in the face of overwhelming odds.

But the decision had to come. Men fighting under the banner of unshakable faith are made of something more than flesh, but they are not made of impervious steel. The flesh must yield at last, endurance melts away, and the end of the battle must come.

Bataan has fallen, but the spirit that made it

stand a beacon to all the liberty loving peoples of the world cannot fail.

The Japanese attitude towards the surrendering battalions of Bataan can best be summed up by an address delivered to European women in early 1942. They were imprisoned on Berhala Island, just off North Borneo:

"You are a fourth-class nation now. Therefore your treatment will be fourth-class, and you will live and eat as coolies. In the past you have had proudery and arrogance! You will get over it now!"

The infamous Death March was next for the defenders of Bataan.

About the surrender of Bataan, MacArthur, safe in Australia, said in his usual grandiloquent style:

"The Bataan force went out as it would have wished, fighting to the end in its flickering, forlorn hope. No army has ever done so much with so little, and nothing became it more than its last hour of trial and agony. To the weeping mothers of its dead, I can only say that the sacrifice and halo of Jesus of Nazareth has descended upon their sons and that God will take them unto Himself."

But the defenders of Bataan, themselves, said it best:

We're the battling bastards of Bataan;
No mama, no papa, no Uncle Sam;
No aunts, no uncles, no cousins, no nieces;
No pills, no planes, no artillery pieces;
----And nobody gives a damn.

American prisoners of war, captured on Bataan peninsula, shown with their hands tied behind their backs, just before they were forced by the Japanese to march in what became the infamous Bataan Death March. The American people back home didn't learn about the Death March until January 1944, almost two years later.

(Top): Colonel James Doolittle, a veteran of World War I, was 45 years old when he led the "Doolittle Raid" over Tokyo. *(Bottom)*: A twin-engined B-25 took off with a load of gasoline and bombs, guided by the white lines on the deck of the USS *Hornet*. Though none of the B-25 pilots had ever taken off from an aircraft carrier before, all 16 B-25s got off without difficulty despite 45-mile-an-hour winds and a rough sea.

Chapter 18
Doolittle's Raid

"I don't want to set the world on fire, just Tokyo."
One of the messages written in chalk on the bombs dropped by Doolittle's flyers over Tokyo

Several events took place between the time MacArthur arrived in Australia on March 17, 1942, and the fall of the Philippines on May 10, 1942.

Ever since Pearl Harbor, President Roosevelt had pressed for a way to bomb Tokyo. By mid-January of 1942, his military commanders had devised a way to accomplish such a task.

Land-based bombers would be launched from an aircraft carrier positioned within reach of Japan's mainland. After dropping their bombs, the bombers would head for the coast of China. General Hap Arnold was all for it. The mission was given to Lieutenant Colonel James H. Doolittle, who spent a month in Florida practicing short takeoffs on land. He and his men practiced, over and over, getting B-25s air-borne within a 750-foot run.

On April 2, 1942, the aircraft carrier USS *Hornet* sailed from San Francisco with sixteen of Doolittle's B-25s and their crews aboard. The *Hornet* was joined by Admiral Halsey's USS *Enterprise* near the launching point 600-700 miles east of Kyushu, one of the four main islands of Japan. The naval force also included four cruisers, seven destroyers, two submarines and two tankers. On April 17, "Task Force Mike," as the operation was called, was twenty-four hours away from launch time.

All went well until 7:30 the next morning, when an enemy craft sighted the task force. After sinking the enemy craft, the decision was made to attack immediately in spite of being 100 miles short of the plan. Doolittle, 700 miles away from Japan, led his bombers off the *Hornet*. Though none of the pilots had ever taken off from a carrier before, all sixteen got off without a hitch, despite 45-mile-an-hour winds and rough seas.

Two hours later, on April 18, Doolittle's bombers were flying in low over Tokyo Bay. After their historic "thirty seconds over Tokyo" bombing, fifteen of the B-25s managed to reach China. The sixteenth, because of fuel problems, was forced to land at Vladivostok, U.S.S.R. Of the eighty flyers on Doolittle's mission, seventy-one eventually returned to the United States.

Why Roosevelt didn't press his military to relieve the defenders of the Philippines or the courageous defenders of Wake Island is something we should all wonder about. If we had been able to hold Guam and Wake Island from the beginning, it would have hampered Japanese plans in the Pacific.

The Emperor's Angry Guest ☐ *III*

Roosevelt and Marshall seemed to prefer symbolic victories in the Pacific up to May 1942.

On May 4, planes from U.S. carriers hit enemy ships in the Japanese-occupied Solomon Islands. May 7-8, U.S. ships sank or damaged eight big Japanese ships in the Battle of the Coral Sea.

On May 10, all remaining American and Filipino forces surrendered in the Philippines. My buddies and I were taken captive by one of the most brutal military machines in history. We would have loved to see sixteen B-25s over Mindanao. Those on Corregidor would have liked to see that too. We would have been heartened by the havoc a nearby American naval force that included two aircraft carriers, four cruisers, seven destroyers, and two submarines would have inflicted on the Japanese military in the Philippines. One of those submarines in the Doolittle task force was the USS *Trout*. What we would have given to know that the submarine that took out the Philippine treasury was back to inflict damage on our aggressors.

Less than a month after the Philippines fell, between June 3 and 6, the U.S. Navy decisively routed the Japanese forces on Midway Island, sinking four carriers, two heavy cruisers, three destroyers, one transport ship and damaging eight more ships. Then on August 7, 1942, U.S. Marines landed on Guadalcanal and at Tulagi on Florida Island in the southeastern Solomon Islands.

A lot of good that did us.

Before General Jonathan Wainwright surrendered the island, marines on Corregidor instructed Filipino soldiers in the use of a machine gun cartridge not familiar to them.

Chapter 19
Back at Del Monte

"We felt like we were on death row waiting for certain execution."
Ralph M. Knox

Our work at Del Monte Airfield was done, so we went back to Carmen Ferry. Morale among the men at Carmen Ferry had been low before, but when we reported that MacArthur had gone to Australia, morale struck rock bottom.

News came to us hot and heavy in the next few weeks, and it was all bad. Bataan had fallen on April 9, 1942. We wondered what the Japanese would do to the buddies we left behind, the ones who had lost the toss. We wondered what would happen next.

Davao and Digos, cities not far away from us on Mindanao, had fallen on April 16. Only two places were left —Corregidor and the rest of Mindanao. The Japanese were getting close to our back door, and we had no place to run. We couldn't send messages home. We didn't have enough to eat.

It was not supposed to happen this way. We were supposed to be in Australia with Generals MacArthur, Brereton and George. With Colonels Eubank and Maitland.

Compare the fate of the highest Dutch military and civilian officials in the East Indies with the fate of the highest American military and civilian officials from the Philippines. Most of the Dutchmen, from their governor-general on down, were ordered to stay behind to share the fate of those they governed when the Japanese defeated them. But American generals, admirals and colonels, along with the highest American civilian official, Francis B. Sayre, fled, leaving their armed forces and civilian population to fend for itself.

It was from guerrillas fighting on Mindanao that we heard about the April 18 bombing of Tokyo by American B-25s from our aircraft carriers. The news made us furious.

The Philippine Islands were the same distance from the U.S. as was Japan. It was another downer.

I cannot be convinced that enough ships, aircraft, and troops were not available to be directed to the Philippines to either aid the defenders on Bataan and Corregidor or to evacuate the Americans caught there. I believe those same planes and ships that were involved in Doolittle's bombing of Tokyo and the other battles could and should have been used to aid the Americans on Bataan, Corregidor and Mindanao. To abandon the Americans and Filipinos in the Philippines, the Dutch in the East Indies, the British in Malaya and leave them there to an uncertain future was a major betrayal.

I know because I was one of the ones abandoned. We felt like we were on death row awaiting certain execution.

We thought about MacArthur safely nestled in Australia with his wife Jean, little Arthur and MacArthur's hand-picked staff officers. Did MacArthur's conscience keep him awake at night? Did he think about the men and women he had left behind?

The post hospital on Corregidor, after the Japanese captured the island.

This photo was taken on May 3, 1942, inside Malinta tunnel on Corregidor, only days before the island surrendered to the Japanese. Statistics after the war show that four out of every ten American POWs of the Japanese died.

The entrance to Malinta tunnel on Corregidor before World War II.

Chapter 20
Fall of Corregidor

"With profound regret and with continued pride in my gallant troops, I go to meet the Japanese commander."

Lt. Gen. Jonathan Wainwright

Immediately after the fall of Bataan, Japanese aircraft and heavy guns bombarded the nearby island of Corregidor, known as the "Gibraltar of the Far East" or simply as "The Rock." For the next 27 days the intensity of air bombardment and heavy artillery never stopped. Corregidor's defenders could do nothing to halt the Japanese onslaught.

Corregidor, shaped like a tadpole, is 3½ miles long and 1½ miles wide at its widest. The tadpole's large head points west toward the South China Sea; its tail points east into Manila Bay and is low, sandy, and wooded. Malinta Hill, with an elevation of about 350 feet, crowns the center of the island, and into it was burrowed the nearly 1,200-foot-long Malinta Tunnel.

At this point in the war, most positions on the island were utterly destroyed. Malinta Tunnel, haven to 11,000 military personnel and 2,000 Philippine civilians, became intolerable with dust, sewage, and heat and humidity. Its narrow hospital corridors were crammed with a thousand sick, wounded, and dying men.

About midnight on May 5, 1942, Japanese troops approached the north shore of Corregidor with assault craft. Fierce fighting raged throughout the night, and the next day more Japanese troops joined the fray. Their tanks headed toward Malinta Tunnel. Wainwright was horrified. He knew his men were outnumbered, emotionally spent, ill-equipped, and lacking in firepower. Like General King on Bataan, General Wainwright decided to surrender. He ordered Brigadier General Lewis Beebe, his aide, to broadcast a message of surrender to Japanese General Masaharu Homma.

Wainwright ordered the American flag to be pulled down and burned and the white flag of surrender to be hoisted. He sent the following message to both Roosevelt and MacArthur. It read: "With broken heart and head bowed in sadness but not in shame, I report that today I must arrange terms for the surrender of the fortified islands of Manila Bay. Please say to the nation that my troops and I have accomplished all that is humanly possible and that we have upheld the last traditions of the United States and its Army. With profound regret and with continued pride in my gallant troops, I go to meet the Japanese commander."

May 6, 1942, at 4 o'clock, the Japanese ferried General Wainwright and several of his staff to Bataan, where they were driven to the small village of Cabcaben to meet Homma. The Japanese documents called for the surrender of all the Philippines, but when Wainwright refused to surrender all the forces, Homma sent Wainwright back to Corregidor to reconsider. Homma told Wainwright that when he agreed to surrender forces on all the islands to inform the Japanese commanding officer on Corregidor, who would then take Wainwright to Manila for a formal declaration of surrender.

By the time Wainwright got back on Corregidor, the Japanese had already entered Malinta Tunnel. He had no choice but to agree to Homma's terms. Wainwright sent a message by plane to General Sharp on Mindanao, explaining the situation. In the meantime, MacArthur had ordered Sharp not to surrender. By May 10, fully understanding the desperate conditions on Corregidor and Bataan, General Sharp had to make a decision.

:cupying Corregidor after the American surrender, Japanese troops crossed the rade ground on their way to the shattered American barracks.

Japanese soldiers shouted "*Banzai!*" next to one of Corregidor's guns after the surrender of the exhausted American and Filipino forces.

Chapter 21
Short End of the Stick

"All we could do was run for it
and fire a few shots as we went."

Ralph M. Knox

Help was not coming. MacArthur was not returning any time soon. General Sharp ordered our unit to proceed to Lake Lanao to dig trenches for the last-ditch effort by the Filipino troops.

On April 16, we left Carmen Ferry for Maramag by truck. Maramag was supposedly the site of a secret air base, but it was only a large grassy field with a road at the end and a woods at the side. In the woods were hidden our few planes, gas dumps, bomb dumps, and quarters for the men. Maramag also had a real hospital, with beds and white linens, a refrigerator, and medicines.

After a few days, we set out from Maramag on foot for the 50-mile trek through the jungle in 100-degree heat to Lake Lanao. We traveled only by day, and the first week we went about 40 miles. We were 100 yards outside a small mountain borough of no more than a dozen grass huts when all of a sudden machine-gun fire opened up on us. Japanese troops occupied the huts! All we could do was run for it and fire a few shots as we went.

The Japanese had anticipated General Sharp's last-ditch effort and beat us to Lake Lanao. Once again we were on the short end of the stick. Instead of backtracking to Maramag, we walked over the Kalatungan Mountains toward the village of Alanib. We arrived on May 7, 1942.

A few days later, a messenger brought us the bad news that Major General William F. Sharp had surrendered. An American P-40 fighter came flying in low, dipped its wings in a friendly greeting, and dropped a parcel on our campsite. In it, a note instructed us to march into Malaybalay and surrender to the Japanese, under a white flag and with the bolts of our rifles extracted.

General Sharp had been forced to surrender all his troops on Mindanao to the Japanese. He was informed that Wainwright's surrender was unacceptable to the Japanese unless *all* forces surrendered and that all American prisoners on Corregidor were considered hostages and would be slaughtered if he did not accept those terms.

General Sharp was in the middle. MacArthur had previously given him a direct order not to surrender, yet Sharp knew Wainwright's position back on Corregidor. So Sharp had accepted the surrender, the Japanese had accepted Wainwright's surrender, and the men on Corregidor were prisoners of war instead of hostages. I was a prisoner of war too, and I was scared to death.

Before we extracted our rifle bolts and waved the

white flag, we had quite a discussion—all of us—about whether it would be better to take to the hills and become guerrillas. Our officers reminded us that, if we did that, we would be deserters. Deserters, we knew, were court-martialed and could receive the death penalty. If I had known what lay ahead, though, as a prisoner of the Japanese, I would have headed for the hills and taken my chances.

We assembled for instructions in surrendering. We were not told what to expect, but had heard about the Japanese threat to open fire on all prisoners on Corregidor, so we had a fairly good idea. Trucks lined up to carry us out. A financial officer arrived in a jeep with a strongbox welded to the side. He was carrying four million pesos ($2 million, American). He dumped the money in a pile on the ground and asked, "Anybody want any souvenirs?" Nobody did, so he set it on fire and burned it.

On May 10, 1942, we boarded our trucks and headed off to Malaybalay to surrender. The lead truck carried our flag of surrender, a huge white sheet mounted to a pole. Malaybalay was only about 25 miles away, but our trip took over two hours. We were in no hurry. We turned ourselves in at a camp that had previously been used by Filipino troops. The Japanese had already surrounded it with several strands of barbed wire and erected a guard tower. The barracks were typical island structures, bamboo with dried-grass roofs. To our surprise, running water was available outside each hut.

As we entered the camp, we each stopped at a table where the Japanese gathered personal information—rank, serial number, outfit. They took our wallets, money, pictures, rings, watches, everything of value. My God! Here I was only 19 years old and a prisoner of war. I had traveled so far to get here, scared beyond imagination, and not knowing if I would survive.

We were turned over to our respective first sergeants, who in turn assigned us to our barracks. There were no beds, just flat bamboo strips to toss our blankets on. Each man was issued a mess kit and a canteen for water.

The Japanese guards were surly. We were exhausted, probably from the six months of abandonment and tension that led to our being prisoners of war. It didn't look good for MacArthur's cannon fodder.

MacArthur, on the other hand, was surrendering himself to something quite different in Canberra that May.

Adulation.

The Australians loved him.

The Australians had always counted on the British Fleet to protect them in time of crisis. They had contributed Australian troops to the British war effort in World War I and were doing the same in World War II.

Now the British Fleet was fighting for its very life in the Mediterranean Sea and Atlantic Ocean. Their battleship HMS *Prince of Wales* and battle cruiser HMS *Repulse* had been sunk by Japanese air power off the coast of Malaya in December 1941.

There were more Australian soldiers in North Africa than back home.

The Australians realized that their salvation lay with the Americans now. All of MacArthur's requests were approved by the Australian government. They dissolved their own military board and turned all of its powers over to him.

They didn't even complain when MacArthur refused to appoint Australian and Dutch officers to his staff, as

Roosevelt and Marshall had suggested.

Except for three officers, every one of MacArthur's staff members were part of the group he had brought with him in March 1942 from Corregidor. We all know how successful they had been in preventing or stalling the Philippine debacle.

History-book photos of the MacArthur family taken during the March through May 1942 period show a happy general and Jean: Breakfast on an Australian train taking them to eastern Australia. Appetizing food on the table. Jean smiling, her coat with a fashionable fur collar draped casually over her shoulders. (I may actually have loaded that coat onto one of their getaway planes.) MacArthur at a session of the Australian parliament in May, smiling, clearly enjoying himself.

The only family member who didn't look well in those early Australian photos was little Arthur. He still looked sick, the way I feel today when I see those photos.

General Douglas MacArthur's son Arthur, with his amah Au Cheu, shown in Australia soon after their escape from the Philippines. Ralph Knox wonders to this day whether the tricycle is one of Arthur's toys he loaded on the third B-17 at Del Monte Field on Mindanao. Instead of taking more personnel out of the Philippines before its final surrender, MacArthur had the third B-17 filled with the personal possessions of his family and officers.

Under Japanese supervision, Lieutenant General Jonathan Wainwright broadcast the surrender of Corregidor and all American-Filipino Forces throughout the Philippines on May 7, 1942.

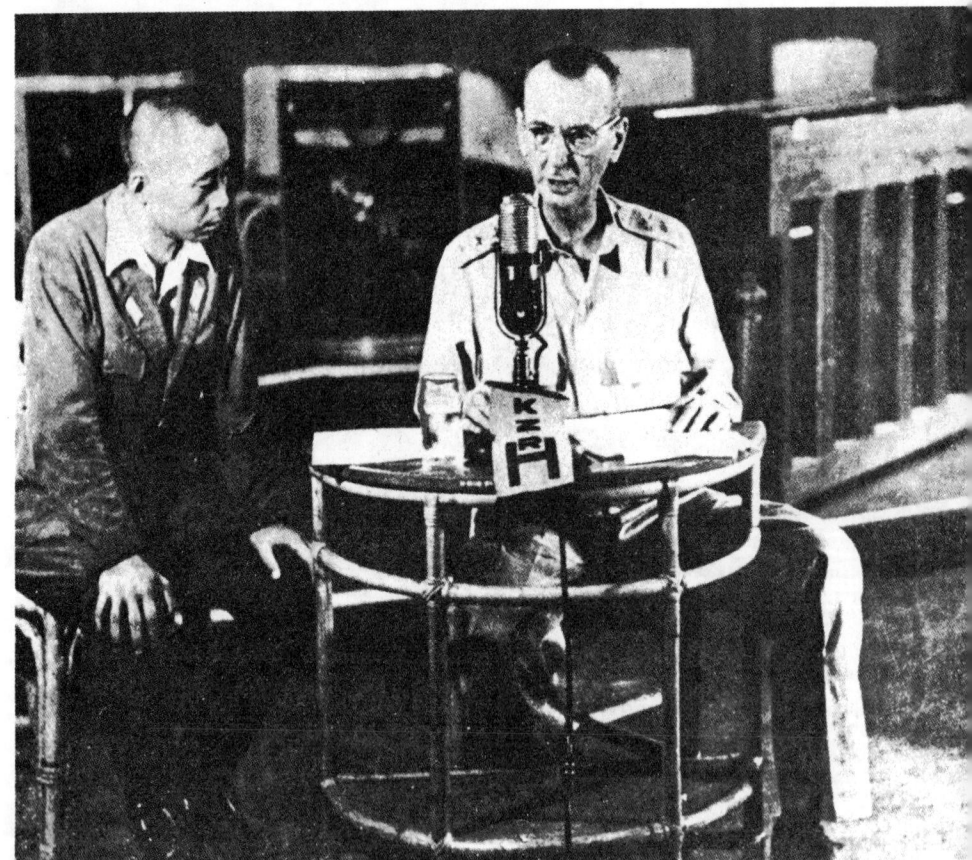

PART TWO

Chapter 22
Count Off

> "It was always 'Speedo! Speedo!' prodded by the constant thrust of their bayonets."
> Ralph M. Knox

The first words of Japanese that we learned were *kiotsukete*, meaning attention, *bango,* meaning count off and *tenko*, meaning roll call. After that we learned how to count.

1: *ichi*	4: *shi*	8: *hachi*
2: *ni*	5: *go*	9: *ku*
3: *san*	6: *roku*	10: *ju*
	7: *shichi*	

In pronouncing Japanese words spelled phonetically with Roman letters, the letter "i" is pronounced like a long "e" and "o" is pronounced as a long "o" only.

If you messed up, you got a rifle butt to the head or back, so we learned real fast. We learned early on to bow when a Japanese guard approached. If we didn't, we'd get another whack on the head. After about a week, everybody had learned to give their *bango* and to bow and things settled down. The Japanese divided us up into ten-man squads, and we stayed pretty much on our toes and close to one another. In the Japanese system, if one person escaped, the rest of the men in the squad would be shot.

Other words we learned were *daikon* for radish, *itai* for hurt, *benjo* for toilet and *takusan* for many. Mount Fujiyama was called *Fuji-san*.

News trickled in from Luzon. None of it was good. We heard about the death marches out of Bataan, how the men marched in the suffocating heat without food or water for days and that those who fell from exhaustion were either bayoneted, decapitated, or shot on the spot by the Japanese. Tales came to us, too, from Camp O'Donnell where 9,000 prisoners were held captive in early April, then moved farther north six weeks later to Cabanatuan, minus the 2,000 who died from lack of food and medicine.

In a way we felt fortunate to be on Mindanao, but we couldn't let our guard down. The Japanese guards put the fear of God in us. It was always, "*Speedo! Speedo!*," prodded by constant threats of their bayonets.

One night in early July, three Americans attempted to escape. They took with them enough rice and canned food to last a week in the jungle, and each carried a bolo for hacking their way to freedom. The three were caught just outside camp and staked to a pole driven into the ground in the center of the camp, in full view of us all. As we prisoners were forced to go about our miserable business around camp, "*Speedo! Speedo!*", the three men broiled in the unrelenting sun. The three, wearing only shorts, were never given any food or water. Their sunburned skin blistered and swelled and cracked. Hordes of large, black flies swarmed around their oozing sores, and after a few days, the men begged to be put out of their misery. A week went by. Finally the Japanese did put them out of their misery, but first they assembled all the prisoners to watch the execution. It was horrible. Tears slid down our cheeks. We prayed. We could see the bullets make dents where they entered the men's bodies and then the blood drain out.

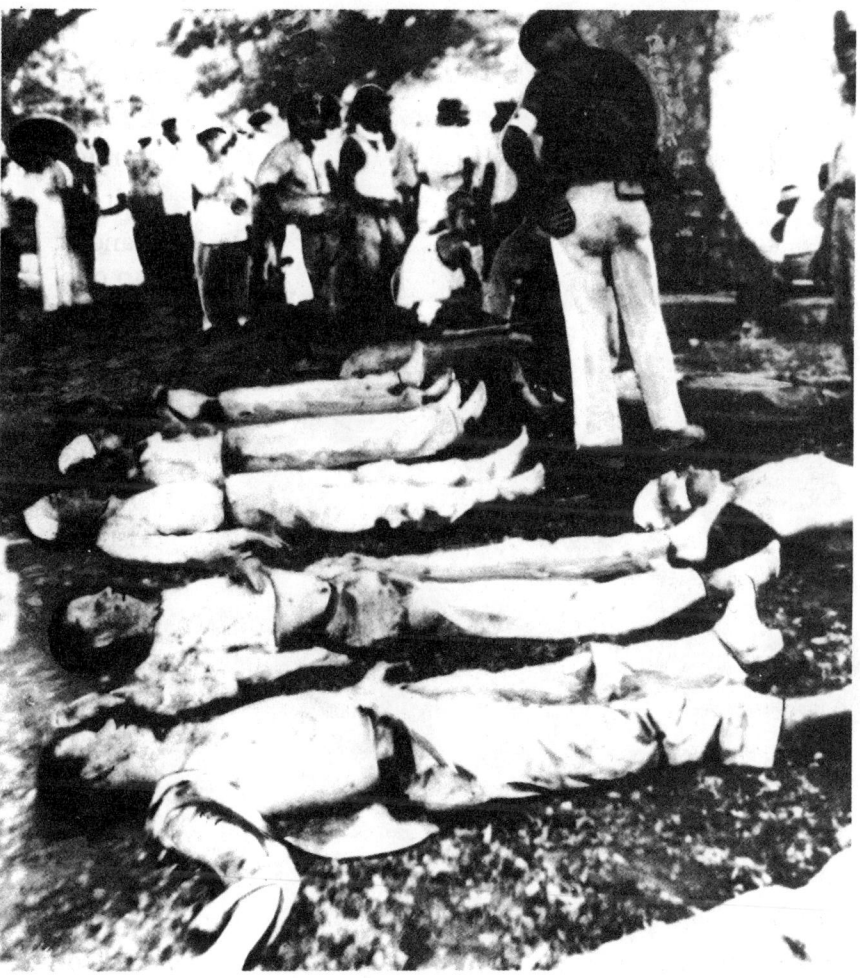

Dead American soldiers were found all along the route of the Bataan Death March.

The Japanese beat, tortured and killed Allied prisoners of war throughout the Philippines, The Netherlands East Indies, China, Malaya, and in Japan itself. Japanese treatment of POWs on Borneo and New Guinea (later in the war) was particularly harsh.

Chapter 23
Hell Ships

"Tyranny, like hell,
is not easily conquered...."
Thomas Paine

Nothing else of that magnitude happened over the next five or six weeks. But there were no good days, and we learned to forget the bad ones. Around the middle of September, rumors flew hot and heavy again: We were going to be moved. Sure enough, a list was posted of 250 personnel, mostly air corpsmen, that were going to be moved to Japan. My name was on the list.

On October 1, 1942, at Cagayan, we boarded the *Ala Maru,* one of the infamous prisoner-of-war "hell ships. The ship sailed north for Manila.

Throughout the war, Allied prisoners christened these rotting, stinking, Japanese tramp steamers with nicknames. *Byoki Maru,* which meant sick. *Stinko Maru. Diarrhea Maru. Dysentery Maru. Benjo Maru* meant floating shit house. According to the Geneva Convention and international law, these ships should have been clearly marked as transporting prisoners. They weren't. Allied submarine commanders who torpedoed them can be forgiven. But not the Japanese.

We sailed past Corregidor four days later as we entered Manila Bay. What an eerie feeling it was to see the Japanese flag waving so high and proud where the Stars and Stripes had flown before. Shortly after we docked at pier 7, the Japanese marched us through the streets of Manila and on to the overcrowded Bilibid prison camp. A few men were left there, crowded in with the mostly civilian Filipino prisoners, but most of us were taken by truck to the Cabanatuan prison camp 75 miles north of Manila and about 50 miles northeast of Clark Field. The night I stayed there, someone said 300 men had died during the night. It rained, and the next morning we could see arms, legs, and other body parts sticking out of the ground. Heavy rain had washed away the dirt from the shallow graves. It was the most sickening sight I've ever witnessed.

After a few days at Cabanatuan, the Japanese took us back to pier 7, put us aboard the *Tottori Maru*, and we headed for Japan. The *Tottori Maru* was another of the many prisoner-of-war hell ships. They crammed about 1,930 of us into the hold, about 20 feet below the main deck. About 275 of us were from Mindanao, while the rest were from Luzon.

When the 15-foot-square hatch was closed, not one speck of air or light could seep through. There were no ventilators, no portholes. We were packed so tightly into the hold there was not enough room to lie down or to even sit, so we sort of half-crouched on the floor. Once a day, rice and watery soup were lowered down to us in buckets. Each man got about one-third cup of each.

We lived in that suffocating darkness for five days

until we reached Formosa (Taiwan), where we were put ashore, stripped, and hosed down to wash off the filth. Hundreds of curious Formosans gathered around the dock to gawk at us, but we didn't care. Modesty, at that point, was the last thing on our minds.

Standing there drying off, I got a good look at the *Tottori Maru*. It was part of a convoy of four prisoner-of-war ships going to Japan and was armed fore and aft with 3-inch antiaircraft guns. It was not marked with the emblem of the Red Cross to show that it carried prisoners of war, as the Geneva Convention required.

Near the end of October, we pulled away from Formosa. The very first day out, the convoy was attacked by an American submarine. One of the ships was hit, so we returned to Formosa. We started out again the next day and the sub attacked again, hitting another ship, so back we went. On the third day, the *Tottori Maru* and the other remaining ship set sail again. Four other prisoners and I were on a work detail, topside swabbing the deck, when all of a sudden loud yelling and screaming broke out. Our first thought was that airplanes had been sighted, but then we realized it was another submarine attack. Two torpedoes were headed directly at us. The *Tottori Maru*'s captain, luckily, made a sudden change of direction and saved the ship.

But who would save the prisoners inside the ship? With so little food and water, we got sicker each day. Everybody had diarrhea. No provisions had been made for latrine facilities in the hold. At first, we didn't even have buckets, but finally four 5-gallon buckets were lowered down to us. Less than two hours later, all four buckets were filled to the brim and overflowing. Requests to empty them were refused. Soon the latrine area was a wading pool of human waste. The stench and the lack of fresh air were disgusting. That and the growing dehydration, hunger, and thirst caused some men to go berserk. They screamed for air and water. At one point some were even trying to suck blood from the dead. They had been driven over the edge and didn't know what they were doing.

The need for water was so acute that many men drank their own urine. Some even drank the raw sewage running in the open drains along the side of the ship. The bodies of the thirty or so who died were hauled topside by tying ropes around their legs or arms, then they were dumped into the sea.

Hell ship was the perfect name for the ship I was on.

On November 7, 1942, our ship arrived at a Korean harbor, probably Pusan. Korea had been a colony of the Japanese since 1910 and they called it Chosen. The prisoners were allowed out of the hold to stand on the dock. Snow was on the ground and the wind howled around the ship. We were barefoot and in shorts, but the frigid air was clean and it felt good. Who cared if we got sicker?

About 50 or 60 Korean soldiers came aboard. They had volunteered to be guards in Japan. The Koreans seemed a superior race to the Japanese, at least in height. All the Koreans on our ship stood over 6 feet tall, were bearded and mean-looking.

On November 9, we arrived at Moji, Japan, on the island of Kyushu across from the main island of Honshu. We were cold, infested with lice, and too sick to eat even if we'd been offered decent food. The two days it took to cross the Sea of Japan had been one tough ride. Enormous waves had washed over the ship and the salty water had seeped through the hatch and drenched us down in the hold.

Our voyage aboard the *Totturi Maru* ended a whole lot better than many of the hell ship voyages later in the war.

The *Nitimei Maru*, with 1,000 POWs on board, was attacked en route from Penang, Malaya, to Moulmein, Burma. Fortunately, most of the POWs were saved.

On November 29, 1943, the *Suez Maru*, transporting POWs, was torpedoed by the USS *Bonefish*, east of Java.

In September 1944, a U. S. submarine sank the *Shinyo Maru*. This hell ship was carrying the last POWs from Mindanao. Many men perished, but Philippine guerrillas rescued 82 survivors.

The biggest hell-ship disaster occurred on September 18, 1944. The *Junyo Maru*, with more than 6,000 Allied prisoners crammed on board, was torpedoed by the British submarine, HMS *Tradewind*. Only about 900 POWs survived. As the ship went down, arguments broke out among the POWs over the nationality of the submarine that sank them.

In December 1944, U.S. carrier planes sank the *Oryoku Maru*. Of the 1,619 POWs on board, nearly 900 perished. The Japanese rounded up the survivors and these POWs continued their journey to Japan in the *Enoura Maru* and the *Brazil Maru*.

Then in January 1945, the survivors of *Oryoku Maru* now on the *Enoura Maru*, were bombed at Takao, Formosa. More than 219 of them were killed. The *Brazil Maru* reached Japan with only about 500 survivors on board from the original 1,619 POWs on board the *Oryoku Maru*.

Sidney Stewart, author of *Give Us This Day*, and Van Waterford, author of *Prisoners of the Japanese in World War*

II, both survived attacks on hell ships and their sinkings. Waterford was only 16 years old when captured by the Japanese on Java and witnessed the Dutch governor-general and General Hein ter Poorten arrive to surrender to the Japanese at Bandung.

When Stewart went overboard to prevent going down with his sinking hell ship, he saw the water was filled with Americans, their pale bodies shining in the dark green ocean.

After surfacing in the water, Stewart heard cries for help from those POWs who couldn't swim. He pretended not to hear those cries. In his weakened condition, Stewart was having enough trouble trying to save himself.

I was lucky to be sent on a hell ship earlier in the war when there was less Allied submarine and bomber activity.

This art depicts the sinking of the Japanese hell ship *Junyo Maru* on September 18, 1944. About 5,500 POWs perished after the unmarked ship was torpedoed by the British submarine HMS *Tradewind*, making it the largest maritime disaster in history. The art was adapted from an old Dutch military publication and is by an unidentified artist.

General Douglas MacArthur and his wife Jean enjoy breakfast on a train to Melbourne, two days after their arrival in Australia. Meanwhile, back in the Philippines, after helping load MacArthur's getaway planes, Ralph Knox and the other volunteers from the 28th Bomb Squadron had evacuated Del Monte. They needed to find food while staying one step ahead of the Japanese. Just days before, the men had loaded onto one of MacArthur's three B-17s several crates of clothes, fur coats, pipe tobacco, and other personal belongings. Being typical young men, Knox and his friends had discovered the contents of the crates while rummaging through them looking for cigarettes.

Chapter 24
Guests of the Emperor

"You are not prisoners-of-war.
You are guests of our emperor."
Colonel Suzuki, Camp Commander, Kawasaki

After marching us nearly naked through the streets of Moji, the Japanese issued each of us a blanket, woolen trousers, a shirt, one set of underwear, and shoes. Those items had been captured from the British in Hong Kong when they surrendered on Christmas Day, 1941.

From Moji, we went to Osaka where we boarded a train for Kawasaki, just south of Tokyo. Along the way, groups of 100 to 150 prisoners were dropped off at various work camps. I and about 150 men went all the way to the end. We were known as Kawasaki War Dispatch Number 5. The camp was just outside Tokyo, near Tokyo Bay and the 7-mile-long Mitsubishi Steel Mill. It was an enormous steelworks with acres of blast furnaces and thousands of workers.

We had barely got settled in our quarters when the guards herded us all outside in a big group. A short, bowlegged man with a mustache stood on a box that made him seem tall and introduced himself. "I am Colonel Suzuki," he announced in perfect English, "your camp commander. You are not prisoners of war, you are the guests of our emperor. You are in the land of sunshine and honey. You will travel to see our beautiful country." He was a lying son of a bitch. The very next morning they force marched us to the steel mill and put us to work.

My number was 601, and I sewed it onto the left side of my shirt. I had my own chop sticks and a bowl, into which I was served a cup of rice three times a day.

We worked from sunup to sundown. The work detail always started with a lineup, *tenko*, the word for roll call, and *bango*, the count-off. Then we marched about ten blocks down the middle of the street. Guards with bayonets fixed on their rifles escorted us. Whenever we could, we picked up cigarette butts off the ground.

Many Japanese civilians worked side-by-side with the prisoners of war at the steel mills. Like us, they were captives. If they didn't work, they wouldn't receive the ration cards necessary for food, clothes, and shelter. Mostly old men and young women, some as young as 14, the civilians gestured in a crude way that their stomachs were empty. In this way they also communicated that they didn't want bang! bang! and made waves with their hands to indicate that they thought we should go home to America. During the Doolittle raid over Japan eight months earlier, the very steel mill that we were now working in was hit by several bombs.

Because of the civilians' doubts about us, we came to work every day, did the jobs we were forced to do, caused no trouble and were friendly to them.

Sergeant Charles Callahan, with us all the way from

Clark Field, handled all our personnel records. He was our go-between with the Japanese, deciding who was too sick to work and who needed medical care. He was a good negotiator and we were lucky to have him.

The Japanese kept the prisoners of war on their home islands for two reasons. One, the prisoners provided desperately needed labor. All of Japan's able-bodied men were in China or fighting throughout the South Pacific. Two, with American prisoners scattered throughout Japan, the Japanese thought the United States would be more hesitant to bomb Japan for fear of killing their own men.

After a day's work in the steel mill and the long trek back to camp, we were exhausted. We ate our meager ration of rice and, for entertainment, we stood around killing the lice and smashing their eggs that lived in the seams of our clothes. If we'd been lucky enough to find a cigarette butt along the road that day, we'd have a nightly smoke before lights out. Rule was, you could smoke only within arms length of the ash receptacle, a tin can nailed to a pole in the center of the building. One night I was smoking a little too far away from the tin can, and a guard caught me. He took me outside and beat the hell out of me with his wide leather belt. He gave me at least 50 lashes across the face, then he made me stand at attention outside the rest of the night. Snow was falling heavily and it was freezing cold.

Work responsibilities at the steel mill varied, from pulling white-hot billets from the furnaces with 7- or 8-foot-long tongs to chiseling defective cracks out of cold billets with a small air hammer. The furnaces were so hot we couldn't stand to work longer than half an hour at a time, and we didn't dare let our pants touch our bare legs.

All through the Dispatch Camps, and in Japanese

144 □ The Emperor's Angry Guest

POW Camps throughout the Western Pacific, Allied prisoners did their best to sabotage the emperor's military productivity. At every opportunity we poured emery dust into axle grease, dropped small machine parts and extra sand into concrete mixes, wound electrical coils in reverse, bolted cylinder heads on too tight or too loose, shook iron filings into generators, took the cotter pins out of the wheels of ore carts, and deliberately drove rivets crooked into the hulls of ships.

At times the civilians would try to communicate with us. They knew no English and our Japanese wasn't very good at first, so we invented a sign language. Mostly, they indicated they wanted the war to be over so they could go back home and get plenty of food. Their food ration was nearly as low as ours. On a good day, a sympathetic civilian might offer us a whole cigarette or share an apple or a bit of burned rice. They had to be careful that the guards didn't catch them, for the guards showed no mercy, not even to their own people.

On December 19, 1942, I was allowed to send a card to my father in Butler, Indiana. He did not receive it until the following summer. Mail came to us about every other month. I received 40 letters the entire time I was a prisoner of war. These were not letters of the usual length. They could only be a few lines long. Six were from my immediate family; the rest were from my Aunt Mildred, a young Michigan teacher.

My folks in Indiana thought I was receiving Red Cross care packages filled with snacks and other good things. After my father received my card in the summer of 1943, Red Cross representatives started collecting $40 a month from my parents, promising that I would receive a monthly parcel. That was a huge sum in 1943, but my father was making good money, including overtime, at the Allison General Motors plant in Indianapolis where they made Studebaker engines for planes. So my family could afford to pay the monthly Red Cross fee. Some of my teachers and family friends had offered to help my parents make the monthly payment, if needed.

I never received any monthly Red Cross parcels. All I ever saw were empty candy-bar and cigarette wrappers.

Prisoners too sick to work in the steel mills were allowed to tend a small garden. It wasn't like the garden my grandparents grew on their Indiana farm, but it served a purpose. The harvested vegetables were added to our watery soup and added a few vitamins to our woefully inadequate diet. The garden was well-fertilized by the "honey dippers." To be more specific, the fertilizer was the human waste from our *benjo*, or latrine. The latrine was nothing more than a cement casement in the ground covered by a wooden floor with three to four holes to straddle and a roof overhead. As the casement filled up, prisoners, or "honey dippers" would scoop out the slop with wooden buckets and scatter it over the garden. There were two important results. One, the white radishes, or *daikon*, grew to be an astonishing 3 or 4 feet long. Two, everybody got dysentery. The most severe cases turned into amoebic dysentery, causing blood and mucus to be passed through the bowels 20 to 25 times a day. Some men lost as much as half their original weight.

We learned to gauge the war's progress by the guards' behavior. The guards became more antagonistic toward us and beat us more frequently and with greater force. We assumed things weren't going well for them. Quite a few times they made us stand at attention all night long. If a prisoner moved even the slightest while at attention, a guard would punish the prisoner by throwing him over his head in a jujitsu exhibition. Each time that happened, we figured they'd had another loss in the South Pacific.

This is a copy of Ralph Knox's short wave message home on October 11, 1943. The Japanese allowed recorded broadcasts by American POWs daily. The message was heard and copied by R. P. Read at Gerard Motors in Hopkins, Minnesota, and forwarded to the families of the POWs mentioned in the broadcast.

DODGE CARS TRUCKS

PLYMOUTH CARS TRUCKS

TEL. HOPKINS 7814-5

GERARD MOTORS
701-703 EXCELSIOR AVENUE
HOPKINS, MINN.

OCTOBER 11, 1943.

THE FOLLOWING IS A REPORT OF A SHORT WAVE BROADCAST RECEIVED DIRECT FROM RADIO STATION JLG-2, TOKYO, JAPAN, ON OCTOBER 11, 1943 AT 10:15 A.M. CENTRAL WAR TIME. THIS BROADCAST WAS ON A FREQUENCY OF 9.505 MEGACYCLES. EVERY DAY THE TOKYO RADIO BROADCAST MESSAGES FROM AMERICAN PRISONERS OF WAR. THIS MESSAGE WAS RECORDED ON A PHONOGRAPH RECORD BY THE PRISONER AT THE PRISON CAMP. THE RECORD WAS THEN TAKEN TO THE TOKYO RADIO STATION AND BROADCAST. THE VOICE ON THE RECORD OF THIS MESSAGE IS THE ACTUAL VOICE OF THE PRISONER. MESSAGE FOLLOWS.

FROM:  RALPH MORRIS KNOX, Age 21, PFC U.S.A. Air Corps, Philippines.

TO: MR. & MRS. HARRY C. KNOX
ROUTE NO. 1,
BUTLER, INDIANA.

MESSAGE: This is Ralph Morris Knox, Age 21, U. S. Army Air Corps, Private First Class. My Home address is Route No. 1, Butler, Indiana, speaking from Prisoner of War Camp No. 5, Tokyo Area, Japan. I would appreciate it if anyone hearing this broadcast would contact my family. Hello Folks - Hope you are listening in. If so this will be the closest we have been since I left home. I am enjoying good health and am being treated well. Hope you and the rest of the family are alright. I haven't heard from you since November 1941 and would like to know how everyone is. How are Robert and Dorothy getting on. I send my best wishes to the rest of the family, Dorothy and friends. Tell them all I hope to see them soon. I would like you to contact the Red Cross and inquire as to what you might send. I hope you have received my three letters written since my arrival in Japan November 11, 1942. Private John W. Durrell of Ordnance Company would like his father, T. W. Durrell of 610 East 12th. Street, Indianapolis, Iddiana to know that he is well and says "Hello Dad". Tell all his friends Merry Christmas and a Happy New Year and he hopes to be home soon. Also - Harry Brewer, 6202 South 39th. Street, Omaha, Nebraska. My fathers address is - Mr. & Mrs. Harry C. Knox, Butler, Indiana. I'll sign off wishing you a Merry Christmas and hoping to see you in the New Year. Your loving son.
Ralph Morris Knox.

See attached sheet for explanation. Receiving conditions were fairly good here today and this record is quite plain although there is some interference caused by a Mexican Short Wave Station. On any correspondence in connection with this message, PLEASE REFER TO THE NAME OF THE SENDER OF THE MESSAGE, DATE OF BROADCAST AND TO MASTER RECORD NO. 346. This message requires a large record. Carbon copies of this letter have been sent to the families of the boys mentioned.

Yours very truly,

R. P. Read.
R. P. Read.

Chapter 25
The Devil for All

> "Be sober, be vigilant; because your adversary the devil, as a roaring lion, walketh about, seeking whom he may devour."
>
> The Bible: I Peter

On Christmas morning in Hong Kong, 1941, a stretcher-bearer saw the Japanese closing in on the hospital and asked an English officer what to do.

"Every man for himself," was the reply.

That sentence should have been emblazoned across the sky throughout the Southwest Pacific in late 1941 and the first five months of 1942. Every American, Filipino, Englishman, Dutchman, Australian, Javanese and Malayan caught in Japan's "Greater East Asia Co-Prosperity Sphere" would have understood.

While I was imprisoned by the Japanese, thousands of other unfortunate men, women and children were suffering too at Japanese hands. Japanese treatment of POWs varied from one island to the next, with Borneo perhaps being the worst place to be captured.

When Corregidor was surrendered in May 1942, one reporter described it as a Gibraltar turned into an Alamo.

In June 1942, the Japanese prime minister, General Tojo announced, "No work, no food!" in regard to all POWs.

In July 1942, 800 POWs died at Cabanatuan in the Philippines.

On August 26, 1942, Western male civilians who had evaded capture by the Japanese by retreating with their wives and children to an old Dutch fort in East Borneo were murdered by the Japanese. Later, the women and children were massacred too.

By September 1942, Koreans were assigned guard duties in most POW internment camps. The prisoners at many camps hated them even more than the Japanese.

In November 1942, the Japanese moved 1,000 POWs from Luzon Island to Davao Penal Colony in the Philippines. Another 1,500 POWs were transported from the Philippines on the *Nagato Maru* to Osaka, Japan.

During the same month, Nichols, Clark, Nielson, and Palawan airfields in the Philippines witnessed the slave labor of 1,800 POWs dispersed to those locations.

By the end of December 1942, a total of 2,545 POWs had died at Cabanatuan.

1943 was no better.

In February, the Japanese sent Baron Hideo Kodama on a fact-finding trip through Japanese-held territories to assess the treatment of POWs. His report was a compilation of complaints by POWs and other internees about how they were being treated. There were no positive changes as a result.

By March, most American and European civilians

were now behind barbed wire throughout the Japanese-held territories.

In late May, the Japanese executed Europeans in East Java who were suspected of anti-Japanese activities. A few days later on the same island, the Japanese executed a group of Dutch Eurasians who refused to join the Japanese-supported native forces.

By September, no Americans or Europeans were walking around free in Japanese-held territories. On September 19, the Japanese rounded up Dutch Eurasians suspected of anti-Japanese activities. Many were imprisoned and executed.

In October, 96 American civilians were executed on Wake Island. They were civilian workers, many of whom had arrived on Wake only weeks before the Japanese attack and occupation.

On October 17, the Burma-Siam Railway was completed. Thousands of POWs perished while constructing the line. Proportionally, more British POWs died than other nationalities and this was later attributed to the poor nourishment the English experienced as children back in England. Proportionally, the nationality with the fewest deaths while working on the railway were the Dutch, most of whom had spent years in the Netherlands East Indies and were more accustomed to survival in the tropics. The Japanese felt that the Australians were the best workers on the railway and the Dutch the poorest. The Japanese had a saying that it took 400 Dutchmen to accomplish the work of one Australian. It wouldn't be the first time in history that a group of slaves pretended stupidity in order to survive.

Two months later, Japanese authorities in Tokyo decided to treat all civilian internees as POWs, except in

Malaya and on Java and Sumatra.

In March 1944, the Japanese decided to move most of the remaining American POWs from the Philippines. Two groups, a total of 500 men, were sent on hell ships to Japan.

Three months later in June, the Japanese moved another 1,200 POWs from Davao to Luzon.

An order was issued December 10, 1944, by Japan's 18th Army headquarters, that Japanese troops were permitted to eat the flesh of Allied dead, but not Japanese casualties.

On March 9, 1945, a documented case of Japanese cannibalism of an American POW occurred. It was reported by a Major Matoba to an American military commission convened in August 1946 on Guam. An order had been given that a Japanese battalion "...wants to eat the flesh of the American aviator, Flight Lieutenant (Junior Grade) Hall." First Lieutenant Kanamuri was in charge of rationing Hall's flesh. Hall's liver was particularly prized by the Japanese, who believed the liver was good medicine for the stomach.

As late as June 1945, the commandant of the Tjideng camp in Batavia (now Jakarta) on Java ordered all food thrown away as punishment for small infractions by the camp's women. The POWs received no food for two days.

By the end of the war, the Japanese had used approximately 160 facilities in Japan to imprison POWs. There were 33 other facilities for civilian internees. These numbers illustrate the extensive efforts by the Japanese to hold Allied prisoners in their homeland and to use them as hostages against an Allied invasion. The Dutch crew and hospital staff of the hospital ship *Op ten Noort*, for example, were internees in Japan from early 1943 to the end of the war. The *Op ten Noort* had been captured after the Battle of the Java Sea with survivors of the sunk Allied warships on board.

At the end of the war, details of Japanese mutilations of live prisoners became known. To this day, many do not believe these accounts, but they have been documented in official records.

A young native woman about 20 years old was found hiding in the grass at Canangay in the Philippines by a Japanese patrol. The officer in charge of the patrol cut off her breasts with his saber and then cut open her womb. She then burned to death in a fire they set.

At Balikpapen, Borneo, a Dutch district officer and a police inspector were forced to converse with a Japanese Army officer. The Japanese officer continually slapped the face and hit the body of the district officer with the scabbard of his sword. Suddenly the Japanese officer drew his sword and hacked off both the Dutchman's arms just above the elbows, and then both his legs above the knees. The Japanese officer then turned to the police inspector and cut his arms and legs off in a similar manner. The policeman struggled onto the stumps of his legs and managed to shout "God save the Queen" before falling dead.

Long before the Iraqi threat of the nineties, the Japanese were involved in the testing and development of biological warfare. Many of the POWs relocated to Manchuria were used in experiments by the Japanese, who were very interested in the development of bacterial clouds. The nature and characteristics of clouds resulting from bacterial dissemination by munitions were studied. In 1944, six million yen (approximately two and one-half million 1944 dollars) were allotted by the Japanese at one research facility alone for this type of work. In one case, a POW was ordered to cut the grass at an experimental site the day after an anthrax trial. He died shortly thereafter.

In *Surrender and Survival: The Experience of American POWs in the Pacific 1941-1945*, author E. Bartlett Kerr assembled the following totals of U. S. POWs captured by the Japanese in 1941-42.

AMERICAN POWS CAPTURED BY JAPANESE

In the Philippines	22,000
On Wake Island	1,555
On Java	890
On Celebes	255
On Guam	400
In China	200
In Japan and elsewhere	300
	25,600

Of the 25,600 American POWs captured by the Japanese at the beginning of the war, 10,650 were dead by the end of the war. Of these, 5,135 died in the Philippines and 3,840 died on Japanese hell ships. The death rate, based on the total Americans captured, was 42 percent. This percentage is about the same as the death rate of American POWs in our Revolutionary War. During the Civil War, only 16 percent of Union POWs and 12 percent of Confederate POWs died after being captured.

In addition to the American servicemen captured by the Japanese in the Philippines, the Japanese also captured 12,000 Filipino Scouts and about 30,000 Filipino troops. About 7,300 American civilians, men, women and children were also interned in the Philippines as a result of the American loss of the islands.

The Japanese held U. S. and Allied civilian prisoners throughout its conquered territory, including women and children. About 4,000 civilian prisoners, mostly Americans, were held by the Japanese on the grounds of the University of Santo Tomas in Manila. Two prisoners are shown here.

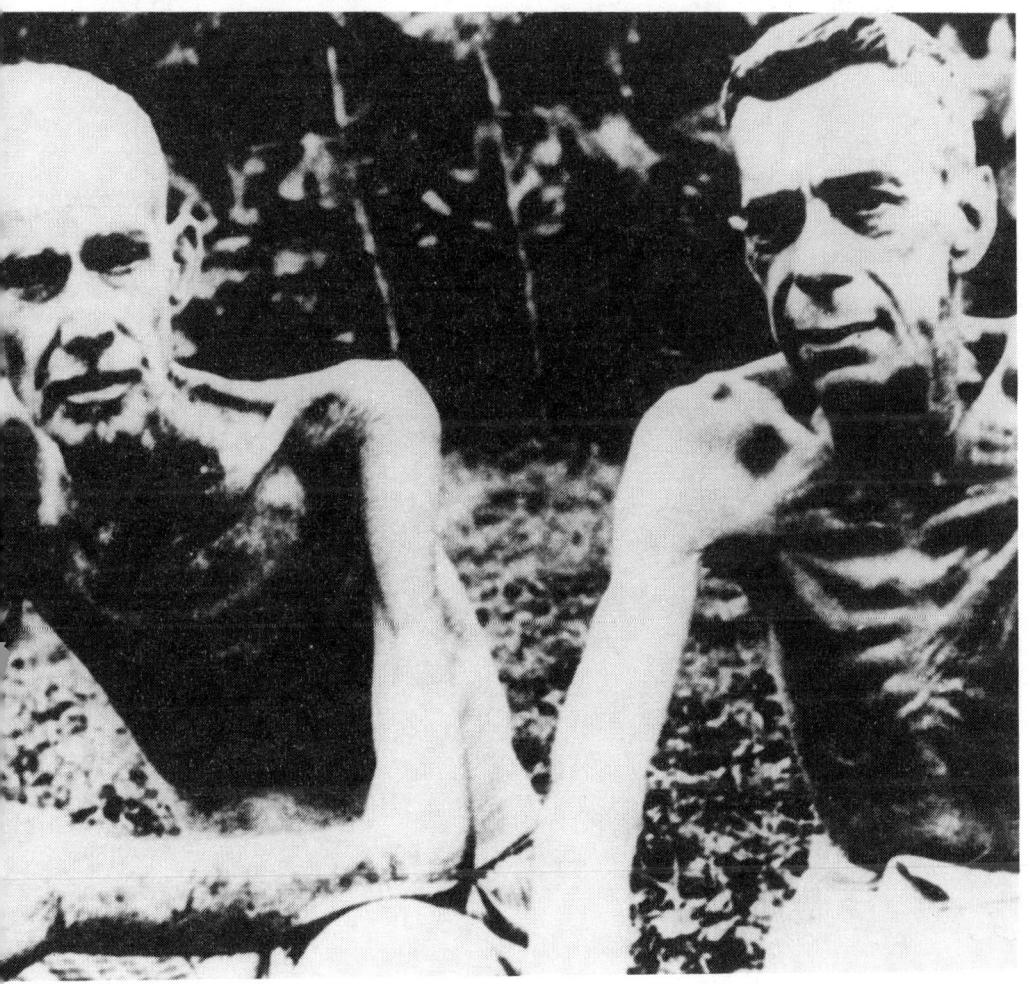

An American prisoner of war at the end of World War II. On starvation rations and suffering from dysentery, he lost over half of his original weight upon capture.

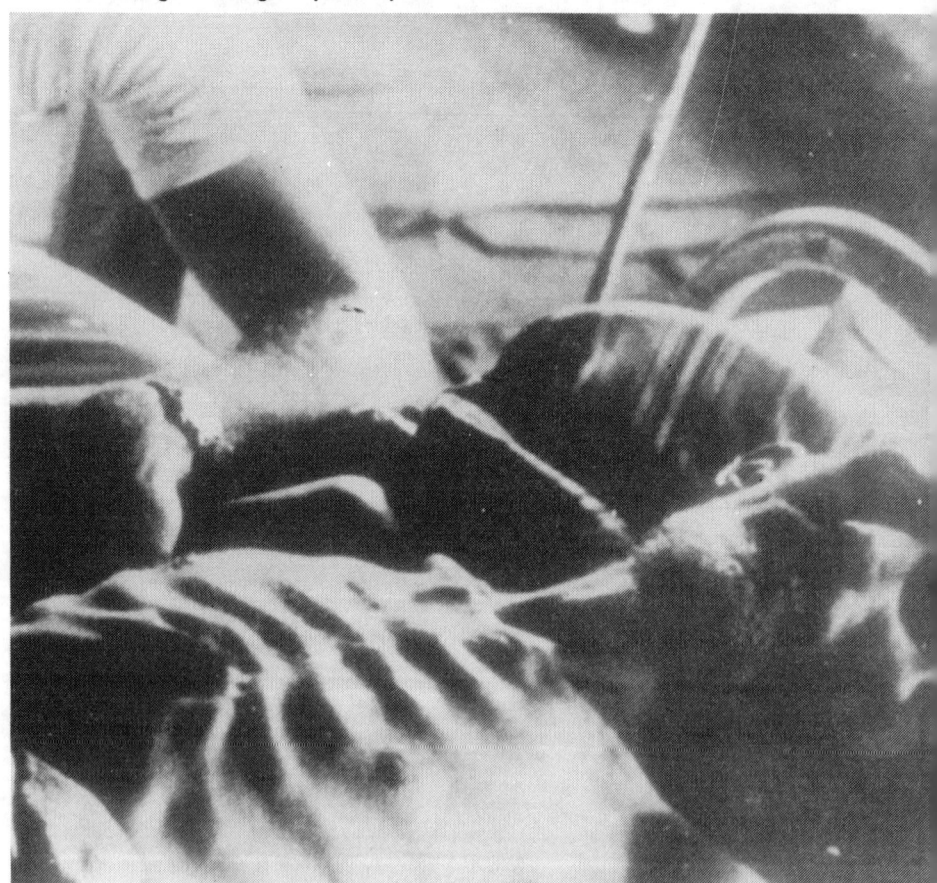

Chapter 26
Sick Bay

> "The Pobble who has no toes
> Had once as many as we
> When they said, 'Some day you may
> lose them all'—
> He replied, 'Fish fiddle de-dee!'"
>
> Edward Lear

On May 12, 1943, I was working outside at the steel mill, assisting in stacking steel rollers that weighed about 2,000 pounds each. A Japanese civilian was tending the crane that lifted the rollers, and I was guiding the rollers into position. As the crane operator lowered one of the heavy rollers, he suddenly swung it over to where I was standing, causing me to lose my balance. My left foot slid under the roller being lowered and the heavy roller crushed my big toe to a pulp and tore the skin off the arch of my foot.

Half an hour after the accident, they took me to the dispensary, where the wound was cleaned and covered with gauze. Someone decided my foot needed more attention, so I was transferred to the Nippon Steel Hospital to be operated on. When I arrived, no surgeon was there to do the work, so I had to wait four hours for one to show up. I was never given any pain medication.

They amputated my big toe on my left foot. I wasn't given any pain medication for that either. I received five stitches on the top of my arch. I was strapped to a table and held down by seven Japanese nurses. I remember screaming when they sawed through the bone. Before I passed out, one of the nurses threw her upper body across me. Her huge, pillowy breasts covered my face and practically smothered me. I woke up the next morning back at camp with a fellow prisoner cradling my head in his lap. I had been in shock all night.

Each day, from then on, I rode in a prisoner-drawn cart to the dispensary to have my foot dressed. In addition to cutting off my toe, the doctor had left a hole in my foot and stuffed it with gauze, supposedly so my foot would heal from the inside out. When the dressing was changed, they pulled out the old gauze and inserted new. I nearly passed out every time.

On May 21, the day after my 21st birthday, I was transferred to the Nippon Steel Camp, and from then on I was taken to the Shinagawa hospital for new foot dressings. I got a new identification number there, too—number 149.

This entire incident was written up for the files on October 31, 1943, by Sergeant Callahan. Addressed to "Whom It May Concern," I still have my copy. Callahan, an enlisted man like me, did his best to record everything. There weren't any of our officers around to look after us.

My foot throbbed constantly, and I kept it elevated as much as possible to try to alleviate the pain. I could always count on a certain Japanese corporal by the name of Shiozawa to visit me periodically. He carried with him a wooden sword, and he never failed to use it to inflict more pain on my aching foot. When he approached me in sick bay, he would ask, "*Itai?*," meaning "does it hurt?" I always responded, "*Takuson!*," meaning "a lot!," to which he would say, "*Itai ni*," or "no it doesn't hurt." Then he would draw his sword and whack it across my foot as hard as he could. The pain was unbearable, and it happened over and over and over again. Each time Shiozawa showed up, it was like the devil himself walked through the door. In the war criminal trials after the war, Shiozawa was classified as insane.

Ralph Knox's Japanese POW number was 149 when this photo was taken. He was assigned a different number at each POW camp he was transferred to.

Another POW made this drawing of Ralph Knox being transported to the Kawasaki camp dispensary by prisoner-drawn cart after an accident at the Mitsubishi Steel Mill resulted in the amputation of his left big toe.

Chapter 27
Hospital Camp

"War is cruelty,
and you cannot refine it."
William Tecumseh Sherman

Finally on November 5, 1943, I was transferred to Shinagawa Hospital Camp. I was renumbered 2064. The number was drawn on cloth and sewn over a piece of cardboard. The cardboard had been cut from a box labeled: packed by the California Prune and Apricot Growers, San Jose, California, and it was pure proof that the Red Cross packages were reaching Japan but not the prisoners.

The 300 sick and dying prisoners at Shinagawa were from the United States and every one of its Allies. I met some good guys there from all over the world.

Everyone at Shinagawa was on half-rations because we couldn't work. We were hungry all the time and had to take matters into our own hands so we wouldn't starve to death. One day, we killed a cat belonging to one of the guards. We put the cat in a bucket, cut its head and tail off and skinned it. Now it looked like rabbit meat. We buried the skin, head and tail. The we added water and greens from around the barracks to the cat in the bucket.

To cook the cat, we took two cans about the size of soup and vegetable cans, put the smaller one inside the larger and removed both bottoms to the cans. We wired them together, connected the wire to a socket and dipped the cans into the bucket of water, cat and greens. The water started to boil instantly. We ate animal protein that night.

The guard was looking for his cat for days.

We had four doctors: Harold W. Keschner from New York City and Leonard Gottlieb from Pennsylvania; Captain Smith represented the U.S. Navy; and Commander Harold L. Cleave was a surgeon from the British Royal Navy. They did the best they could under the circumstances.

In addition to my smashed foot, I was being treated for amoebic dysentery, starting sometime in 1944. Off and on for nearly a year, I had severe abdominal pain and intense diarrhea. At my worst, I passed blood and mucous 20 to 24 times a day. The doctors gave me emetine, carbasone, and finally, yatren, but nothing worked. By April 24, 1945, I was gravely ill, so Dr. Cleave performed an exploratory laparotomy, without anesthesia. He looked around inside my gut, saw no perforations, took out my inflamed appendix, and sewed me back up. I remember passing out from the pain, waking up and passing out, again and again.

Once when I was awake, Dr. Cleave, after noting my low white cell count, had asked me, "How the hell can you be alive with this cell count?"

In his August 17, 1945, report about the operation and my condition, Dr. Cleave wrote: "...parts of the intestine were very inflamed and thickened. The walls of the gut felt rubbery or fleshy, and were quite double their normal caliber.

He made a slow convalescence."

After the operation, I got worse. After two blood transfusions directly from Dr. Keschner's arm into mine, the severe cramping began to ease and I could eat a little and sleep. I slowly regained strength. I was in the hospital for nineteen months.

I played chess at Shinagawa. I had carved a chess set out of the branches of trees and played other prisoners as often as possible. In 1952 I received a letter from one of the ex-POWs whom I played with regularly, George Galletti, an Italian ship captain.

"Are you still playing chess?" Galletti wrote. "I remember that you were regularly winning when you were playing with me at Shinagawa."

Galletti was captured by the Japanese after he sank his merchant ship in Hong Kong harbor when Italy changed sides and became an Allied nation instead of Axis in 1943.

The concentration required to play chess allowed me to briefly forget my constant pain and miserable surroundings.

A Japanese interpreter in military uniform by the name of H. Koyanaji visited the hospital. We talked about the missing Red Cross packages, and he readily admitted that the guards had confiscated practically all of them. When the interpreter found out I was from Indiana, he asked if I knew Bill Fox, the sports editor of the *Indianapolis Star*. I had heard of Bill Fox. Anyone who ever participated in sports back in Indiana knew of Bill Fox. It turned out that, before the war, the interpreter had lived with the Fox family as a houseboy. He asked me to say hello to the family when I went back home and wrote all the family members' names on the back of his name card. He had more confidence in my survival at the time than I did.

I saw Bill Fox after the war and told him about this meeting with his former houseboy. He wasn't pleased that he had harbored a future Japanese soldier in his home.

Also after the war, I learned that Red Cross supplies supposedly reached POWs in December 1942, December 1943 and December 1944 in time for Christmas each year. While those parcels were distributed in many camps, I never received any.

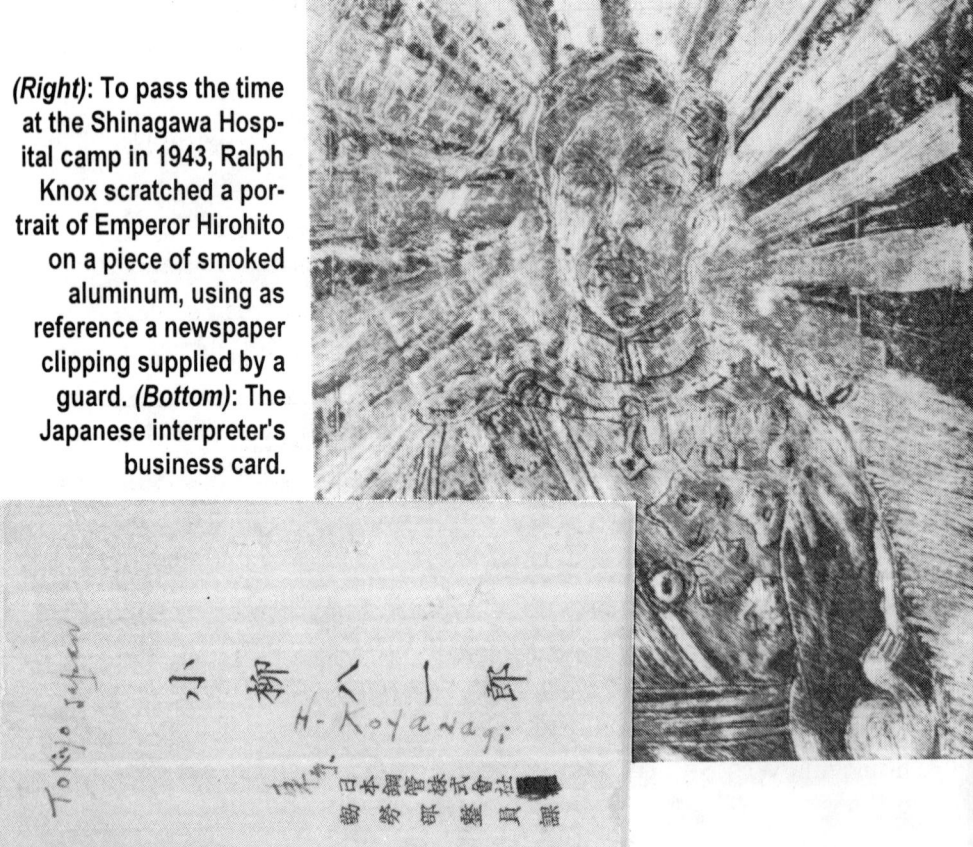

(Right): To pass the time at the Shinagawa Hospital camp in 1943, Ralph Knox scratched a portrait of Emperor Hirohito on a piece of smoked aluminum, using as reference a newspaper clipping supplied by a guard. *(Bottom)*: The Japanese interpreter's business card.

Chapter 28
B-29s Firebomb Tokyo

> "Then conquer we must,
> for our cause it is just."
> — Francis Scott Key

We knew the end was coming soon, but we could not fathom how it would end. American B-29 bombers had no problem penetrating outer defenses to reach their targets over Japan. We prisoners were witnesses to that. Even as early as the end of May 1945, more than 500 planes hit Tokyo right outside our camp. The pilots had no way of knowing we were there. Just like the hell ships, the prisoner-of-war camps weren't marked. We thought sure we'd be killed by our own bombs. Over half of Tokyo was destroyed and more than 200,000 of its civilians were killed. One million were left homeless.

General Hap Arnold, Army Air Force Chief-of-Staff back in Washington was on record as saying: "Japan has sowed the wind, now let it reap the whirlwind."

It did.

The B-29s were four-engine aircraft, capable of twice

the performance of the B-17s. They were 100 feet long, 28 feet high and had a wing span of 142 feet. B-29 armament included twelve 50-caliber machine guns with a 20-mm cannon in the tail. The planes flew at 350 miles per hour, had a range of 3,500 miles and could carry 10,000 pounds of bombs.

Each time the B-29s flew over Tokyo, we prisoners were ordered out of the barracks and into the foxholes we had previously dug. Our camp was near Tokyo Bay and just a few feet above sea level, so our foxholes were always full of water. The Japanese guards forced us to jump in anyway, prodding us, *Speedo! Speedo!*, into the holes with their fixed bayonets.

One night near the end of May, hundreds of B-29s hit Tokyo with incendiary bombs. By this time the Japanese' defenses were reduced to nearly zero. When our planes flew in to deliver their bombs, they met little opposition. The fire from the bombing was intense and the light was so bright that we easily could have read a newspaper at our camp, if we'd only had one.

No official news came to us. All we knew was what we saw, and it looked bad for the Japanese. At times it looked bad for us prisoners too. When the bombers came in low, we prayed they'd miss us. Eventually we got brave enough to stand outside and wave at the incoming planes. We didn't bother to get into the watery fox holes anymore, and the guards were too scared to force us.

As the American and other Allied Forces were steadily retaking Pacific islands from the Japanese and closing in on the Japanese home islands, the Japanese guards continued to take their fear and frustrations out on the prisoners. They'd hustle us out of the barracks, line us up, and beat the hell out of us.

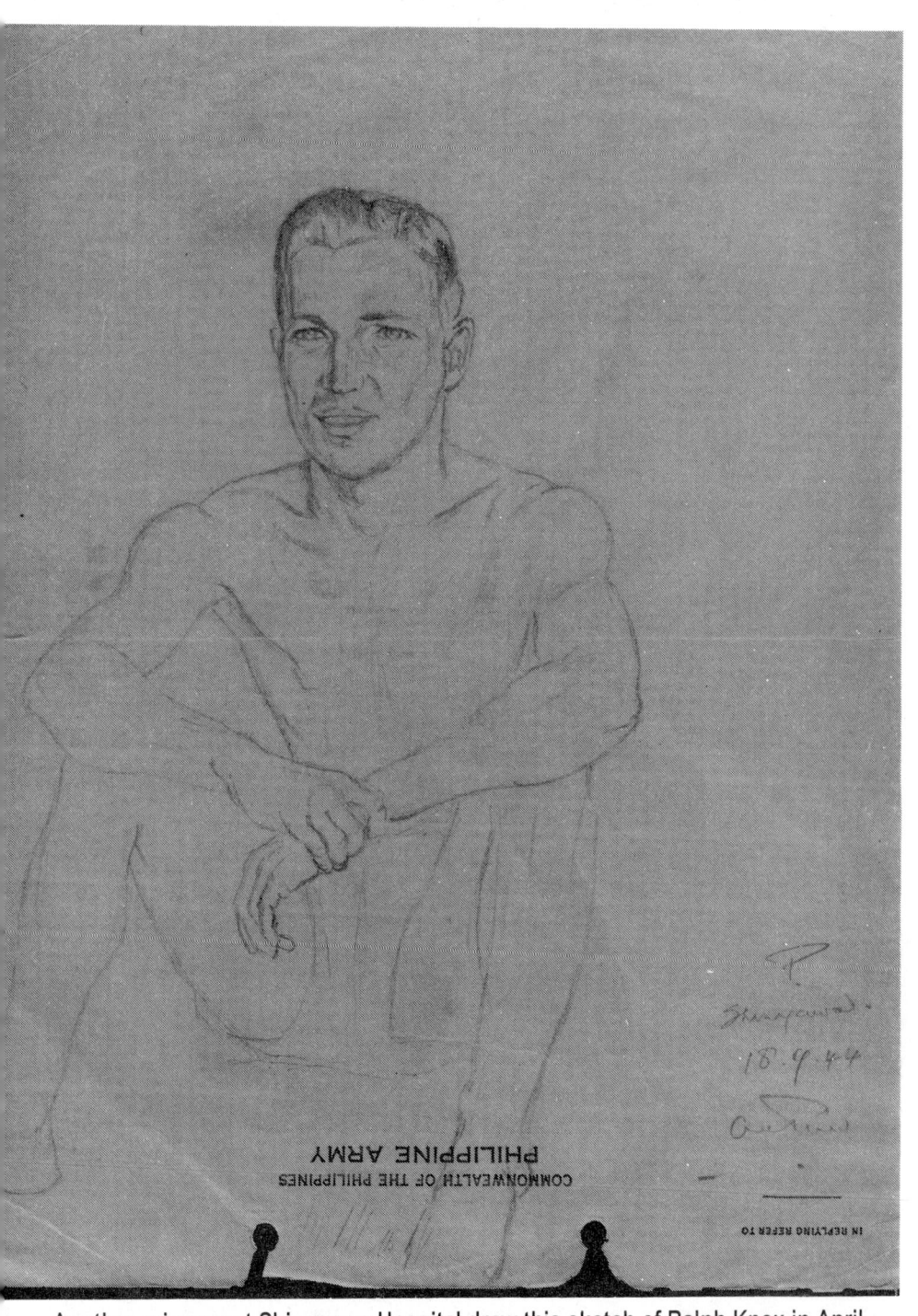

Another prisoner at Shinagawa Hospital drew this sketch of Ralph Knox in April 1944 on a piece of paper from a notepad of the defeated Philippine Army.

After the last shots had been fired in World War II, captured Japanese officials admitted that the B-29 Superfortress, more than any other weapon, had caused their defeat. On the one night of August 1, 1945, 801 B-29s bombed the Japanese homeland.

Chapter 29
Hiroshima and Nagasaki

"We are warning you to flee."
Text from leaflets dropped by B-29s over Japan

August 6, 1945, was a day like any other at our prisoner-of-war camp—more beatings, less rice, more sun, no news. We didn't know it was a day that history would never forget. We didn't know until much later that Colonel Paul Tibbets lifted the *Enola Gay*, named for his mother, off the tarmac at Tinian with a crew of 12 men and dropped the biggest damn bomb imaginable onto Hiroshima. That uranium bomb, named "Little Boy," killed over 80,000 Japanese.

Then three days later, Major Charles Sweeney and his men in a bomber called *Bock's Car* dropped an even bigger plutonium bomb called "Fat Man" on Nagasaki. About 100,000 people were killed in that city. Nagasaki had actually been *Bock's Car*'s secondary target. The city of Kokura, the site of an arms factory, and now a suburb of Kitakyushu on the northern coast of Kyushu island, was too clouded over for *Bock's Car*'s crew to drop their bomb.

Kermit Beahan, the bombardier on the B-29 that dropped the plutonium bomb on Nagasaki, recalled the bombing in an interview with *The Houston Chronicle*. "I saw a mushroom cloud bubbling and flashing orange, red and green. It looked like a picture of hell. The ground itself was covered by a rolling black smoke. I was told the area would be destroyed, but I didn't know the meaning of an atomic bomb."

Our first inkling of what had happened came a few days later when B-29s dropped informational leaflets all over Japan. Hundreds of the pieces of paper fluttered down to our prison camp. In Japanese, the front side of each leaflet read:

To the people of Japan: Don't you think you want to help your own family members and friends live? To help them, please read this leaflet carefully.

In a few days, four or five of the cities shown on the back, where ammunition is being made, will be destroyed by American planes. In order for the war to end fast, we plan to destroy these.

We don't know where they will fall. Also, we don't like to hurt the innocent. Therefore, please leave these cities. We are not enemies of children and families. Your real enemies are those making these military places.

We would like to provide a way for you to escape from these militants and make a better Japan. Do you want peace? Besides these cities, other places may also be destroyed but of these cities, at least four will be destroyed.

We are warning you to flee.

On the pamphlet's reverse was a picture of four or five B-29 bombers and the names of ten more Japanese target cities:

Ujiyama	Nagaoka	Uwajima	Koriyama
Kurume	Oamori	Habodate	Tsu
	Ichinomiya	Nishiromiya	

Finally Emperor Hirohito spoke to his people. "I cannot bear to see my people suffer any longer. It pains me to think of those who served me so faithfully, the soldiers and sailors who have been killed or wounded in far-off battles, the families who have lost all their worldly goods, and often their lives as well. The time has come when we must bear the unbearable. I swallow my tears and give my sanction to the proposal to accept the Allied proclamation."

The Emperor couldn't bear to see his people suffer any longer! Can you imagine? But he had the stomach to see the Americans, English, Dutch, Australians and Chinese suffer.

Even several years after the war was over, when Hirohito started traveling on goodwill visits to Britain and the Netherlands, for example, there were demonstrations against him and the nation he represented. He and the Japanese deserved to know that civilization had not forgotten.

Hirohito's birthday was celebrated each year on April 29. The Japanese government distributed photos of the emperor on his birthday after the war to mark the occasion, showing him working in his palace garden. It seemed he was a good gardener. But, of course, Japanese soil would be richer after the war. It had been fertilized with the blood and bones of "the Emperor's Guests" from around the world.

As to whether our dropping of Atomic bombs on two Japanese cities was justified, I think we have to examine the records of events of that time. Japanese troops in the field fought blindly on, even though the Japanese managers of its war knew they could not defeat the United States. Nearly 150,000 Japanese soldiers perished on New Guinea.

The struggles for other Pacific islands were also horrific. The defense of Saipan cost the lives of almost 60,000 Japanese military and civilian personnel.

The figure includes about 4,000 Japanese women and children who committed suicide by leaping from cliffs rather than be captured by the advancing Americans. Those women and children had been encouraged to sacrifice themselves by Japan's radio stations who were repeatedly broadcasting these lines from an ancient Japanese poem:

Across the sea, corpses soaking in the water,
Across the mountains, corpses heaped upon the grass,
We shall die by the side of our lord.
We shall never look back.

Events of the months before August 1945 confirmed to Allied leaders that the Japanese would defend their homeland just as vigorously as they had defended Saipan. Allied leaders did not know that Japanese troop strength in Japan was as weak as it was.

POWs on Sumatra and on other islands had been ordered by their Japanese guards to dig huge pits that were to be their graves if the Americans attacked. As a former prisoner of war myself, I can imagine the despair of those POWs.

The war needed to be brought to an immediate end.

On August 8, 1945, Russia declared war on Japan, only two days after the big bomb fell on Hiroshima and only two weeks before Japan surrendered. Nonetheless, Russia claimed her full rights as a belligerent.

Japan accepted the ceasefire, which took effect at 7 a.m. on August 15, 1945. The day before, 450 B-29s from the Marianas had bombed Tokyo. The night before the cease-fire, 560 planes hit Tokyo, and just prior to the surrender, 145 planes bombed the Nippon oil refineries at Akita, Japan.

(Top): "Little Boy," detonated over Hiroshima on August 6, 1945, was 28 inches in diameter, weighed 8,900 pounds, and was equal to 20,000 tons of TNT. *(Bottom)*: "Fat Man," dropped over Nagasaki August 9, 1945, was 60 inches in diameter, weighed 10,800 pounds, and had about the same destructive power as Little Boy's.

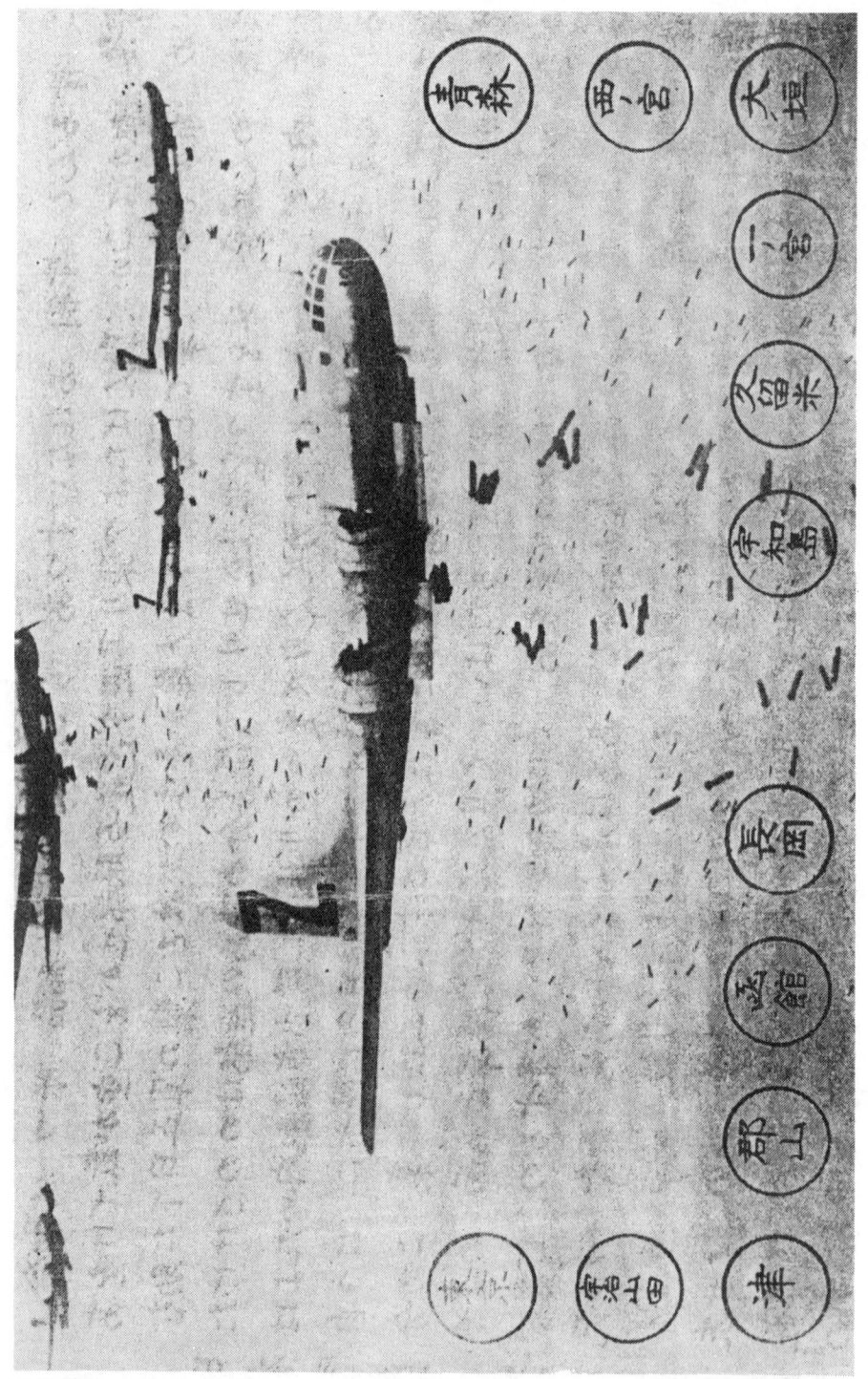

The back of the leaflets dropped by B-29s all over Japan after the atomic bombs were dropped on Hiroshima and Nagasaki. Inside each circle was the name of a Japanese city that was considered a future target for atomic bombing. The text on the front of the leaflet promised that at least four more cities would be destroyed.

Chapter 30
Stassen the Liberator

"When do we shoot the guards?"
A U. S. Marine upon release
from a Japanese POW camp

August 15 was known as change day for the Japanese soldiers guarding the prisoners of war. At prison camps scattered all over Japan, the once gung-ho, sadistic guards simply threw down their rifles and ran home.

The next day planes came looking for us. Fighters from Navy aircraft carriers flew low missions over the land trying to locate the prison camps. It wasn't hard to find us. We were outside waving our hands in the air like lunatics. As the pilots spotted us, they dropped packages of cigarettes to us. The packages floated down to the ground on little parachutes. Attached to the packages were tags giving the pilot's name and address. After that, B-29s came in and dropped 50-gallon drums loaded with food, shoes, clothes, and toiletries. Some of the drums slammed into the barracks, and at some camps, the drums went right through the roofs, striking and killing prisoners. From the parachute silk, we cut out letters and arrows and laid them on the ground to spell out messages to the pilots and to give them directions for dropping supplies.

One of our messages said, "Pappy Boyington is here." Colonel Gregory Boyington was a Marine fighter pilot who was shot down somewhere in the Pacific and picked up by the Japanese and interned in our camp. Before he was shot down, however, he had shot down 28 Japanese aircraft. If the Japanese had known that, they probably would have left him in the ocean for the sharks.

On August 28, 1945, the battleship USS *Missouri* sailed into Tokyo Bay to accept Japan's surrender. The next day, the prisoners of war at Shinagawa were rescued. A landing barge loaded with U.S. Marines led by Commander Harold E. Stassen came ashore and took us all away. I weighed 89 pounds and was on crutches. My foot was still giving me fits, but I was the happiest Hoosier alive that day.

I'll never forget how huge those marines looked to me —their clean uniforms, their clean smell—as they came ashore to liberate us. They placed us aboard the USS *Benevolence*, a hospital ship anchored out in the bay. It was on its maiden voyage and was spic and span. We hadn't seen anything that clean in years. First, they took away our filthy, vermin-infested clothes. Next we took a bath and put on new khakis.

Freedom was strange at first. After all, I had been a prisoner for 40 months. I hadn't even been a citizen of the United States during that time because once a soldier waves the white flag of surrender, that soldier automatically gives up citizenship of his country and becomes a ward of the country he surrenders to.

My first meal was a poached egg and a thin slice of toast. I couldn't get it all down. It was too rich for my system after eating nothing but rice for over three years. My stomach could handle the ship's homemade ice cream, so ice cream was my diet for the first few days.

From the hospital ship, we could see the battleship *Missouri*, where the signing of the Japanese surrender was consummated on September 2, 1945.

Japan was represented at the signing by Foreign Minister Shigemitsu, among others. His credentials from Hirohito, when translated, were a flowery four paragraphs:

"*Hirohito,*

"*By the Grace of Heaven, Emperor of Japan, seated on the Throne occupied by the same Dynasty changeless through ages eternal,*

"*To all to whom these Presents shall come, Greeting!*

"*We do hereby authorize Mamoru Shigemitsu, Zyosanmi, First Class of the Imperial Order of the Rising Sun to attach his signature by command and in behalf of Ourselves and Our Government unto the Instrument of Surrender which is required by the Supreme Commander for the Allied Powers to be signed.*

"*In witness whereof, We have hereunto set Our signature and caused the Great Seal of the Empire to be affixed.*

"*Given at Our Palace in Tokyo, this first day of the ninth month of the twentieth year of Syowa, being the two thousand six hundred and fifth year from the Accession of the Emperor Zinmu.*"

Two thousand six hundred and five years since the first emperor of Japan! The Japanese had their borders closed for most of that time to exclude any outside influences, especially western influences. This left their feudal society pretty intact right up to the war. The God-Emperor was on top as a figure-head, his name used by autocratic governments such as General Tojo's to justify their laws and enforce the discriminations they imposed. When the Japanese started flexing their military muscle in the thirties, they brought all that with them as baggage to the countries they conquered. It's no wonder their soldiers beat men, women and children. That's the way they had been treated. The God-Emperor stood for all of that. But finally, because two atom bombs had been dropped on them and a huge army was about to storm their beaches, the God-Emperor couldn't stand to see his people suffer any more! What hypocrisy! The real purpose of that flowery language was to keep the God-Emperor and the autocrats in power. The entire God-Emperor system was designed to keep people suffering and the Japanese would have installed that system throughout Southeast Asia if we had let them.

That's what all that flowery language from the Japanese Royal Court really meant.

When I was leaning against the railing of the *Benevolence*, looking across at the *Missouri*, I had no idea that my Uncle Robert was on the battleship, frantically looking for me. Robert Earl Nowels was my mother's brother, a Lieutenant Commander in the navy. From January through September 1945, he had been in command of the *LST 1038*. He asked for leave and permission to board the big battleship in order to learn about my whereabouts. Instead, he became a witness to the Japanese surrender ceremony.

Shortly after the signing, the *Benevolence* sailed 25 miles south, separating me even more from my uncle. We docked at Yokohama. I don't know how the Red Cross managed to get there before we did, but the first thing we saw were Red Cross tables lined up selling coffee, cigarettes, candy, and other items we had only dreamed about for so many months. Selling these things to prisoners of war liberated only a few days before! On down the pier, however, the Salvation Army had set up tables, too, but there was a big difference—the Salvation Army gave us the stuff free.

Each ex-POW had been given $200, but that didn't mean I wanted to throw mine away. After being incarcerated for so long, it took me only a short while to realize that the dollar wasn't worth what it had been on December 8, 1941.

It was on the docks at Yokohama that I saw 20 to 30 Allied POWs who had been exposed to the devastation of the atomic bombs at Hiroshima and Nagasaki. One side of their faces and bodies looked normal. The other side had been exposed to the bombs and radiation. On that side, their flesh looked burned and uneven. The skin appeared to be rippled. I, but by the grace of God, could have been one of them. I silently prayed for those men.

Ex POWs were not allowed to venture away from the pier. Those in charge thought we might try to avenge our captivity and torture by harming Japanese civilians.

Nothing was farther from most of our minds. The Japanese government had already done them enough harm. All we wanted to do was go home. I'd had my fill of the Japanese.

Lieutenant General Jonathan Wainwright and Lieutenant General Sir Arthur Percival watch General Douglas MacArthur sign the Japanese surrender document aboard the USS *Missouri* on September 2, 1945. Wainwright had surrendered Corregidor and Percival had surrendered Singapore to the Japanese in 1942. Shown at the far left is Vice Admiral C. E. L. Helfrich of the Dutch Navy. In early 1942, Helfrich had urged that the American and Dutch Asiatic fleets confront the Japanese on the high seas.

Chapter 31
Return to the States

> "Such is the patriot's boast,
> where'er we roam,
> His first, best country ever is, at home."
> Oliver Goldsmith

In a few days, after the runways were repaired, I was bound for home in a huge Army Air Force Skymaster. Our first stop was the tiny island of Guam. Greeting us at the bottom of the stairs as we deplaned were Red Cross nurses, a few of whom offered their bodies to us for $50. They didn't get any of my money!

During the overnight stay on Guam, I sent my first international cable by Western Union to my parents back home in Indiana: "Rescued. See Soon." Then we boarded the Skymaster for our nonstop flight to San Francisco. It was a long and laborious flight, but when we flew over the Golden Gate Bridge and Alcatraz in the bay, I was rejuvenated. I was home! My prayers had been answered, and my spirit was still strong. My faith had sustained me for those hellish, interminable years.

We were taken by bus to Letterman General Hospital.

Doctors there examined us, but the facility seemed incapable of dealing with so many men who had been imprisoned for so long under such horrible conditions. Hospital personnel were mostly interested in finding out where our homes were so they could ship us off to a military hospital nearby.

I was at Letterman General for about ten days. I received daily dressings on my foot, and was issued a partial uniform. A records department was set up to reconstruct our military records that had been destroyed during the raid on Clark Field almost four years earlier. We were bombarded with questions about serial number, places and dates of duty, campaigns we'd been involved in, wounds, date of capture, and medical disorders. They needed the information to establish which honorary medals we were entitled to.

At a ceremony on the grounds of Letterman General Hospital, I was awarded 12 decorations:

    1. Purple Heart
    2. American Defense Ribbon, 1 Bronze Service Star
    3. Victory Medal, World War II
    4. American Theater Operation
    5. Asiatic Pacific with 2 Bronze Stars
    6. Good Conduct
    7. Three Presidential Citations
    8. Air Medal with O.L.C.
    9. Philippine Defense Medal
    10. Philippine Presidential Unit Citation
    11. AAF Air Crew Member Badge
    12. Distinguished Unit Badge with 2 Bronze O.L.C.

Normally, it's easy for a soldier to be awarded a Good Conduct Medal. But I think all of us POWs really earned that one this time. I've always wondered whether General

Douglas MacArthur received a Good Conduct Medal.

It would have seemed logical that the doctors, especially psychiatrists, would have been curious as to how we had survived the ordeal with the Japanese, but nobody on the medical staff ever asked. They didn't care. They just wanted to get rid of us. To be fair, all we wanted was to get home. It would take a while for POWs to realize that while we might be okay physically, psychologically, we might never recover from what we saw and suffered.

Later we learned that very few POWs who had beriberi in Japanese prison camps reached the age of 60. Too often, ex-POWs died unexpectedly or from what a coroner's report says is "heart attack." Not just American ex-POWs, but British, Dutch, Australian, and Filipino ex-POWs too. Coincidence? No way.

Letterman General Hospital ceremony, at which former POWs were awarded medals. Ralph M. Knox is sixth in line from the left.

UNITED STATES HOSPITAL SHIP
★ BENEVOLENCE ★

The battleship USS *Missouri*, shown after World War II, and the hospital ship, *Benevolence*.

PART THREE

Chapter 32
Back Home Again in Indiana

> "Mr. Dove was shocked that
> I didn't know where my parents lived."
> Ralph M. Knox

After the awards ceremony in San Francisco, I flew nonstop to Fort Sheridan, Illinois, and from there in a twin-engine DC-3 to Camp Atterbury, just outside Columbus, Indiana. That I was back on my home turf became quite clear when I got to the U.S. Army's Wakeman General Hospital. The hospital was in the middle of a cow pasture!

On my first walk alone down the hospital's main corridor, I encountered the father of all bastard officers. I was on crutches, no belt, no necktie, and wearing a house slipper on my disabled foot. The officer stopped, stuck his face up close to mine and yelled, "Don't you know you're supposed to salute an officer. You're out of uniform. What're you doing out here?"

My first reaction was total surprise and then I got mad, but I gathered my wits about me and said, "Well, sir, it's like this. If you were where I was for the past 40 months and never issued a set of G.I. uniforms during that time, you probably wouldn't be in proper dress code either."

At that he mellowed and invited me into his office. He was Colonel Blocker, Wakeman's administrator and chief surgeon. Nobody had informed him that a former prisoner of war was being sent to his hospital. He asked where I had been imprisoned, for how long, and how long it had been since I'd seen my parents. When I told him, he immediately issued me a seven-day pass and a car and driver to take me home, 175 miles away. Colonel Blocker wasn't such a bastard after all.

I didn't let my parents know I was coming. I wanted to surprise them, but I didn't actually know where in Butler they lived. They had moved since I'd been away. The driver and I arrived in Butler around 8 p.m. Most of the sidewalks in the little town were rolled up, but luckily, Dovey's Diner was still open. I had known Mr. Dove most of my life. His son had been a good friend of mine. A couple of customers were inside the diner drinking coffee and shooting the breeze. As soon as I walked through the door, Mr. Dove recognized me. He jumped over the counter and gave me a big bear hug.

Mr. Dove was shocked that I didn't know where my parents lived, so he said, "I'll take you home. I wouldn't miss this for the world." His two customers were amazed that he would leave his business unattended.

My family and I had a wonderful reunion. They were truly overjoyed to see me but clueless as to what I or any of the men in the Philippines or the Pacific had gone through.

Apparently the real news about the American prisoners of war held by Japan had been suppressed, probably even deliberately censored by our government in order to protect those leaders in Washington who had carried out the "Europe first" strategy. MacArthur's bosses in Washington had even directed him to silence the words of prisoners of war who had escaped. Men who had been fortunate enough to escape from the Philippines to Australia were ordered not to relate the details of the Bataan death march or of their treatment in Japanese prison camps to the Press. So, back then, the American people were unaware of the atrocities their sons, fathers, uncles, and brothers had suffered at the hands of the enemy.

I learned to keep my mouth shut because when I answered most of the questions asked me, the people who asked them reacted with disbelief. I later learned that this was a common reaction by people at home to the stories of ex-POWs in many countries. Sigrid Heide, Norwegian author of *In the Hands of My Enemy*, had been held in two German concentration camps. On her way back to Norway through Sweden at the end of the war, she found the Swedes laughing at newsreel footage of the concentration camps, saying there had to be a limit to this "devilish Allied propaganda."

I was quite a curiosity in Butler, as popular as a sideshow in a traveling carnival. Nosy relatives and family friends bustled in and out of our house. They had never seen a prisoner of war before.

Instead of treating me as a war hero during that week, my family acted as if I was the same 17-year-old, immature boy I had been when they last saw me. At first it was okay, but after a few days I began to resent it, and our relationship began to unravel.

Life had continued for them, but for me it had stopped in 1942. I wasn't the same person. I had missed too much. I felt like an alien from another planet or like Rip Van Winkle waking up after his long sleep. While I was in Japan, I hadn't even learned that President Roosevelt had run for and won a fourth term and then died. I knew nothing about Harry S. Truman, our thirty-third president.

When my seven-day pass was up, I encountered more anxiety and pain back at Camp Atterbury. Colonel Blocker operated on my foot and tried to make it look as normal as possible. In the time since the accident, the other four toes on my left foot had settled at a strange angle. They stuck straight up. Colonel Blocker put steel pins in them to hold them down, then he pulled the skin of my foot over the gaping wound where my big toe had been. Finally, he grafted a 4- by 5-inch patch of skin from my upper left thigh to cover a hole on top of my arch, the hole the Japanese had stuffed with gauze so it could heal from the inside out.

The day after the operation I was in excruciating pain, but it didn't matter to the army orderlies who came through with their mops and buckets of soapy water. They made me get out of bed and mop the floor under and around my bed. This was a daily occurrence and brought back memories of Shinagawa.

Two months later, I got another pass to go home. Off I hobbled on my crutches with steel pins protruding from the ends of my toes. It was encouraging to be able to leave the hospital, but no matter where I went, I couldn't get away from the pain.

By this time, my three brothers were home and discharged from the service. In Japan, I hadn't known they were off fighting. News of the draft board and of the ration system hadn't reached me. Robert, my oldest brother, joined the Flying Tigers in China, later taken over by the Army Air Corps. Charles, two years younger than me, wound up in the Air Corps too, in Europe. My youngest brother, James, quit high school to join the Navy and served somewhere off the coast of China. James eventually finished high school in 1948, one year after my sister Alice and she was three years younger. Because my mother had four sons who served the country during wartime, she received four stars, which she proudly displayed in the front window of our house.

My health began to improve considerably and eventually I was out of the hospital more than I was in. I went to Camp Atterbury for a day or two at a time to have the dressings on my foot changed. Otherwise, I was at home in Butler.

Congressman Gillie, from Fort Wayne, invited me to be his guest in Washington, D.C., for a day. I gladly accepted and spent the day with him as he went to committee meetings and voted in Congress. He introduced me to his colleagues, and we ate lunch in the Congressional dining room. I felt like a big shot on crutches.

One evening I took a date, Hanna Lewis, to a night club in Newport, Kentucky, across the Ohio River from Cincinnati. She wore a stunning black formal gown and a beautiful pearl necklace, and I wore my military dress uniform with all my ribbons on display. A stranger came and sat at our table. At first I thought he was trying to put the make on Hanna, but after we talked for awhile, he said he wanted to paint my portrait. He was Montgomery Wells, the celebrated painter of the beautiful blondes in the Breck Shampoo advertisements and on the Breck Shampoo bottles. I sat for Mr. Wells on three occasions while he painted my portrait in full military dress.

Time came for the steel pins in my foot to be removed. I dreaded it, and the experience turned out to be a hundred times worse than I had imagined. Again, it reminded me of Shinagawa. First, the dried-out bandage was pulled off to expose the surgeon's handiwork. The bandage didn't want to come off; it clung like a burr to the hardened blood and partly-healed, tender tissue of my foot. Next came the steel pins that were holding down my four toes. As soon as the pins were pulled out, the toes popped right up in their familiar, upright position. The medical staff saved the worst for last—the stitches. The patch of skin from my thigh had been stitched to the top of my foot with 70 tiny, black stitches, and by now, they had healed and were ingrown. The orderly didn't care. He dug down through the tender skin of my foot until he found all 70 of them and pulled them out one at a time.

Portrait of Ralph Knox by Breck Shampoo artist, Montgomery Wells.

Chapter 33
Discharged and Deserted

> "There is no discharge in that war."
> Ecclesiastes 8:8

I was discharged from the army twice. To this day, I do not understand why. My first discharge was on July 10, 1946 at Fort Sheridan, Illinois. Right after being discharged, at Fort Sheridan, the army transported me to the hospital at Wright-Patterson Field in Dayton, Ohio where I was immediately reenlisted. I spent the next ten months at that hospital. My second and final discharge was on May 19, 1947, from Wright Patterson Field.

My Certificate of Disability for Discharge from Wright-Patterson included a long list of ailments: duodenal ulcer, irritable bowel syndrome, anxiety disorder, degenerative joint disease of part of my spine, a ventricle hernia and neurosis. Physically, it listed the amputation of my "left great toe with callus plantar surface and arthritis, plantar scar at amputation site of left great toe, traumatic ankylosis of the second, third, fourth toes of left foot," and a right hip scar. I celebrated my twenty-fifth birthday the next day.

I was an angry and bitter man. Not once was I ever offered a consultation with a psychiatrist, a psychologist, or other mental-health expert. I had been only 19-years-old when abandoned by my country on a tropical Philippine island thousands of miles from home. I had suffered the worst imaginable human injustices and indignities. I felt more than ever that I and all my fellow prisoners of war in the Philippines had been sacrificed by Roosevelt and MacArthur and their cronies.

I was fighting mad, and I had lost respect for authority. I felt the world owed me a living. After all, I had been a prisoner of the Japanese for 40 months, and I'd lost six precious years of my youth.

I left the army with nearly $10,000 back pay, a lot of money in 1947. What does every young man do when he has a wad of money in his pocket? Buy a car! And that's exactly what I did. I went to see C. J. Maxon, the guy who wouldn't let me borrow one of his old used cars for high-school graduation. The first thing that popped out of his mouth was, "Oh, no. I can't sell you a *new* car. There's a long list of farmers and merchants waaaay ahead of you."

As I said before, I was fighting mad. I argued my side of the story. I reminded him that I was off at war while he and all those farmers and merchants were back in the States safe and sound and making money.

I eventually bought a new 1946 two-door Buick a few months later, ahead of any of the farmers, but only after I put up a $500 cash bond to the local American Legion Post.

The same thing happened when I wanted to buy my mother a new refrigerator from Oberlin Appliance Store. They had a preferred list, too. It didn't include returned G.I.s.

My mother and I were shopping downtown Butler one day and ran into Mrs. Oberlin, the store owner's wife. Sadly, she had lost her only son in the war. Joe Oberlin, a Navy pilot, had been shot down somewhere in the Pacific. I knew Joe. We had played basketball together in high school. When Mrs. Oberlin saw us, she blurted out to my mother, "Why couldn't it have been one of your sons? You had four in the service, and they all came back. I had only Joe." My mother almost collapsed right there on the spot.

My days of being a prisoner haunted me. I'd been caged like an animal, starved, beaten, tortured. Night after night in prison, I had doubted I'd see the next sunrise. But I had survived. I was beginning to wonder why I bothered.

Now back home, did anyone care? Nobody asked how it was, how I felt, what I was thinking. Maybe they cared but were hesitant to pry into the past. Maybe they didn't want me to remember the bad stuff. Maybe. But I needed to talk about it. I needed help, but help never came. I just muddled through the best I could.

There was no work in Butler for me, so I went to Fort Wayne to work for Farnsworth-Capehart Company as a material control planner on the Talos Missile Project. My two bosses there, Frank Cawley and Andy Perry, took special interest in me and helped me deal with my anxiety and nervousness. Their attention helped reduce the intensity of my anger, got it to a level I could manage, though nothing could ever take the anger away completely. It was always with me, like the slight limp I walked with for so many years.

Over time, the anger began to work in my favor. It became stimulating instead of debilitating, giving me a slight edge over others, and I became successful. I worked hard, and the harder I worked the more my mental anguish receded into the background.

My work took me to several electronics companies, all associated with government electronics defense contracts. My specialty was starting military divisions in those companies. I eventually started my own company, Knox Electronics, in Kansas City, Missouri. To get along, I had to deal with the corrupt system of government contractors and commercial contracting officers or purchasing agents. To get information and contracts, one had to continually give out fur coats and vacation trips to destinations such as Spain. I always saw a little bit of Colonel Suzuki or Corporal Shiozawa or Roosevelt or Churchill or, even, MacArthur in the people I dealt with.

I also began documenting what had happened to American POWs in the Philippines, the Far East and Japan. I have collected documents and articles about the subject for over 50 years. It has helped channel my anger into positive activities, but also fed my anger when I learned something about the unfairness of what had happened to POWs during the war in the Philippines and Japan, compared to the Japanese rehabilitation after the war.

For example, General Minoru Genda, as a commander in the Japanese navy in December 1941, was directed to draft the air tactics for the Pearl Harbor assault. Though illness kept him from piloting a bomber over Pearl Harbor, he was considered responsible for originating the low-flying attacks by torpedo bombers on our battleships.

After World War II, he was commissioned a general in the Japanese air force. In 1962, he received the highest United States honor given to foreigners, the Legion of Merit for his role in rebuilding the Japanese air force and for cooperating closely with the United States.

In 1969, this Legion of Merit winner, General Genda, indicated that if he had been commander-in-chief of Japanese armed forces in 1941, he would have ordered repeated air attacks on Pearl Harbor, occupation of the Hawaiian Islands and attacks on the U.S. west coast from bases in Hawaii. Not surprisingly, his comments were protested by American veterans' groups. I don't wonder why!!

When Katsu Tojo died of a heart ailment in her Tokyo home after the war, her obituary offered some insight as to what had happened to that privileged, autocratic class of Japanese that brought death and misery to the Pacific. She was General Hideki Tojo's widow. General Tojo had been hanged as a war criminal in December 1948.

Mrs. Tojo had been living a secluded, private life since her husband's execution. She had declined to appear in public and turned down all requests for interviews. "I am a person of the past. Please leave me alone," she would say.

However, her son Teruo Tojo was president of Mitsubishi Motors Corporation at the time of her death. That means that Tojo's family, even though he had been executed as a war criminal and they had enjoyed a privileged life-style because of his position during the war, did not suffer any major reverses after the war.

General Tojo's son was head of Japan's second-largest auto firm when his mother died! This was the same company that manufactured Japan's Mitsubishi Bombers during the war. Those bombers had a distinctive sound as they flew, described by some as the Mitsubishi moan. Yet the war criminal's family thrived afterwards, perhaps even more so than during the war.

Appointing a son of Adolf Hitler to be the head of Volkswagen after the war would be a comparable injustice.

When I pass a Mitsubishi auto dealer, I'm the one who moans now. One of the reasons I moan is because, economically, American veterans of World War II did not fare as well as the Tojo family. Two economists in 1990, Joshua Angrist of Harvard University and Alan Krueger of Princeton University produced an analysis of World War II veterans. Published as a working paper by the National Bureau of Economic Research, it shows that World War II veterans had earned about five percent less than their contemporaries in the decades after the war.

The Angrist-Krueger analysis makes use of the fact that World War II draft boards drew on the pool of men in simple chronological order of their birth. Approximately 75 percent of the men born in the first six months of 1926 served with our military in the war. After that year, the probability declined quarter by quarter so that just 22 percent of those born near the end of 1928 ever served.

But younger workers earned more after the war than veterans, strongly suggesting that military service in World War II was generally a handicap for the returning soldiers, sailors and airmen.

Thousands of returning World War II POWs from the Philippines have suffered from physical ailments for decades as a result of their treatment by the Japanese. I have had stomach ulcers all these years and the arthritis in the small of my back was caused by my limp.

However, the families of the Pacific War's top Japanese criminals did just fine, thank you very much.

In 1952, the U.S. government War Claims Commission was offering a maximum of $1.50 to former POWs for each day they were used as slave laborers or treated inhumanely by the enemy. For his 40 months as a POW of the Japanese, Ralph Knox qualified to receive about $1,800.

WAR CLAIMS COMMISSION
WASHINGTON 25.

MAY 23 1952

Mr. Ralph M. Knox
610½ N. Main St.
Apt. #1
Mishawaka, Indiana

Dear Sir:

Reference is made to your recent letter concerning Public Law 303, 82nd Congress, approved April 9, 1952. Insofar as former prisoners of war of World War II are concerned, Public Law 303 provides a maximum benefit of $1.50 to prisoners of war for each day they were forced to perform labor and/or were subjected to inhumane treatment, in violation of the Geneva Convention of 1929 regarding the treatment of prisoners of war. In the event of the death of the prisoner of war, certain survivors may claim in his stead.

Claims must be filed on official forms. The War Claims Commission is drafting regulations and preparing claims forms governing these claims. The Commission is working as rapidly as possible to complete this work and to make claims forms available for early distribution. When available, the claims forms will be obtainable through the American Red Cross, the Veterans Administration, State Veterans Agencies, recognized veterans organizations, or directly from the War Claims Commission, Washington 25, D. C. or its office in Manila, Republic of the Philippines. The War Claims Commission also plans to mail claims forms directly to all persons who have filed claims under the War Claims Act of 1948, as amended, pertaining to the $1.00 per day benefits for violations of the Geneva Convention relative to food rations. An announcement will be made as soon as claims forms are printed and available for distribution.

Your cooperation in awaiting the Commission's announcement during this period will be greatly appreciated.

Sincerely yours,

F. Byrne Austin
Executive Director

WCC 169

(*Left*): Ralph Knox, shown upper right, and his three brothers, all served in the military during World War II. Robert Knox is upper left, Charles Knox is lower left, and James Knox is lower right. (*Right*): Ralph Knox posed with his aunt, Mildred Nowels, after the war. His aunt sent him the most amount of letters while he was a POW.

Chapter 34
Return to the Philippines

"Which is worse,
the inhumanity of the Japanese
or the helpfulness of the Americans."
Carmen Guerrero Nakpil, April 23, 1967 issue of the
Manila Sunday Times Magazine, referring to brutal
American assault to free Manila, February 1945

In early March 1967, almost 20 years after my military discharge, I received a call from Harry S. Truman's secretary asking if I would come to Independence, Missouri. The former president wanted to talk to me.

Naturally, I went. He asked me several questions about how the Japanese had treated me during my captivity. Neither of us said a word about the two atomic bombs he ordered dropped on Japan in 1945. He talked about the upcoming pilgrimage planned by the American Defenders of Bataan and Corregidor. The survivors were returning to the Philippines in April to commemorate the 25th anniversary of their capture by the Japanese. Truman's staff had done its homework, for he knew that I was one of the youngest prisoners of war in Japan.

As one of the youngest prisoners and now a Missouri businessman, President Truman asked me to hand carry a letter to President Ferdinand Marcos of the Philippines. The letter was written in behalf of all the former prisoners returning for the commemoration. I didn't hesitate to accept such an honor.

For the next several days, I was on cloud nine at Knox Electronics. I bought a new suit, two new pairs of shoes, new luggage, a movie camera, a still camera, and I called everybody I knew.

I even called on Harold Stassen in Philadelphia, when I was there on a business trip shortly after my meeting with former President Truman. Because Stassen was the man who had liberated me and the rest of the prisoners from Shinagawa, I have always held him in the highest respect. I went to his law office and personally invited him to return to the Philippines for the Bataan and Corregidor pilgrimage. He said he would consider it, but on March 17, I got a letter from him with his regrets. He could not make the trip.

On March 28, 1967, I went back to Independence, Missouri, to pick up President Truman's letter. Along with the letter, typed on his letterhead, he gave me an autographed photograph of himself.

Coming from a president who had personally fought for his country, in World War I in Truman's case, this letter has always meant a lot to me.

"Dear Mr. Knox,
I would appreciate it if you would convey to all who will have gathered to commemorate the 25th anniversary of

the American Defenders of Bataan and Corregidor my warm and grateful greetings—and a respectful salute for their courageous and great service at a critical time in the life of this nation."

It was signed, *"Sincerely yours, Harry S. Truman."*

On April 3, I boarded a chartered, 15-hour Northwest Orient flight to Manila from O'Hare in Chicago. It had been a busy last few weeks reaching this point. Even *Life* magazine had been in touch with me. The editor wanted me to act as a consultant to their photographer who would be taking rolls of historic photos.

Conveniently, the photographer and I were staying at the same hotel. He was very young, very naive, and like so many young people, lacked basic knowledge of World War II. He followed me around like a chick follows a mother hen, taking hundreds and hundreds of pictures.

The photographer went with me to President Marcos's office to record my meeting with him. Marcos was busy with official duties at the time, but when he learned my reason for being there, he took a short break from his work to accept the letter from Truman. He promised to read it aloud at the Luneta grandstand on Sunday, April 9, following the military parade.

We Defenders of Bataan and Corregidor marched through the streets of Manila. We took a bus trip to Bataan. All along the way, Filipinos, wearing colorful native dress, lined the streets. Little children had made flags for the occasion, and they waved them as we made our way along the route. School girls, wearing the same style dress, lined up in all the villages along the route. As their dresses were a different color from village to village, the girls made a very festive site.

It was a beautiful, touching journey.

On Bataan, we gathered at kilometer 0, where the infamous Death March began, and again at kilometer 105, where it ended. We traversed the winding road to the Altar of Freedom on Mount Samat, a shrine dedicated to those who died on Bataan. President Marcos, his wife Imelda, and their three children went too.

Edgar D. Whitcomb also made the journey to Manila for the 25th anniversary of the American Defenders of Bataan and Corregidor. Ed was to become the governor of Indiana from 1969 through 1973. But I had met him many years ago back at Clark Field when he was a navigator on a B-17. Ed wrote a book about his experiences escaping from the Philippines, entitled *Escape From Corregidor*.

One of Ed's friends had a little jingle that he sang while they were at Bataan in 1942:

"How ya gonna keep 'em
Down on the farm
After they've seen Bataan?"

When Ed had heard on Bataan that General MacArthur was to leave them for Australia, he reacted with a shrug: "MacArthur's presence or absence meant little to us, since so few of us had ever so much as seen him."

MacArthur had not visited the front lines at Bataan often. He preferred the safety of Corregidor at that time and, everybody knew it.

I took the time to visit Clark Field during the trip. Nothing was familiar. Even the runways were now concrete.

On a side trip to Hong Kong, I went to Kowloon and spotted some sort of shrine made of white marble with a red carpet leading up some stairs where there was a bust of Mao Tse-Tung. Thinking it would make a good picture, I proceeded up the stairs with my movie camera when, all of a sudden, I was surrounded by Chinese police dressed in black uniforms. Shouting at me, they confiscated my camera. Damn, I thought I was going to be a prisoner of war again! I got the hell out of there as fast as I could.

In many ways, this was a personal pilgrimage for me. I hadn't been back to the Philippines for 25 years. Many tremendous changes had taken place in the islands since the Japanese had forced me aboard a hell-ship in 1942.

Some of the changes were superficial. In December 1941, Manila's movie theaters were showing "It Started With Eve," starring Deanna Durbin, Charles Laughton and Robert Cummings. "Rookies on Parade," a Republic Picture starring Bob Crosby and Ruth Terry, started its run in Manila on December 24, 1941. Two days later, Manila would be an open city and none of the American soldiers, sailors or airmen in the Philippines could have been considered rookies by that time. We were all seasoned veterans fighting for our lives.

In 1967, they were still showing American movies in Manila. Elvis Presley pictures were popular.

The obvious major change was that the Philippines were now a truly independent nation. No Americans such as Francis B. Sayre were running the civilian administration and no American generals such as MacArthur were in charge of the Philippine military. The Filipinos were proud of their independence.

One thing that hadn't changed was the close relationship between the Americans and Filipinos even though the United States had let the Philippines down during the war. The Filipino soldier and scout had fought alongside American soldiers under the American flag in 1941-1942. By not defending the Philippines properly in 1941-1942, Roosevelt and MacArthur allowed the islands to be ravaged by the Japanese for three years. Manila was destroyed during its liberation in February 1945. So many buildings had been burned and shelled that American troops could see from one side of the city to the other. Japanese troops had dragged drums of gasoline into buildings to torch them.

By the time of the liberation, 125,000 Filipino civilians had been killed. Filipino men, women and children were beaten if they did not bow to Japanese soldiers during the occupation.

In 1985, I received the Bronze Star and Citation dated March 22 for meritorious achievement 7 December 1941 to 10 May 1942. I actually received the award 43 years after it had been authorized by the president, by executive order August 24, 1962. Former Congressman Richard Roudebush presented me the award at VFW Post 673 in Jasper, Indiana.

In 1986, the U. S. Department of Defense authorized and established the Prisoner of War medal. I received mine from a good friend, Congressman Lee H. Hamilton, in a special ceremony at the nation's capitol in Washington, D.C. My sister Alice and her husband were with me at the ceremony. I've known Lee since 1962. He was in Congress from 1964 until he retired at the end of 1998.

One individual who has helped me in recent years is John Hickey, Director of Rehabilitation of the American Legion in Indianapolis. I owe all that I'm now receiving in entitlements from the Veterans' Administration to him.

(Left): Signed photo given by former President Harry S. Truman to Ralph Knox.
(Lower Left): Knox presented former President Truman's letter to Philippine President Ferdinand Marcos, noting the 25th anniversary of the fall of Bataan and Corregidor.
(Below): Truman's letter to Knox.

HARRY S TRUMAN
INDEPENDENCE, MISSOURI

March 28, 1967

Dear Mr. Knox:

I would appreciate it if you would convey to all who will have gathered to commemorate the 25th Anniversary of the American Defenders of Bataan and Corregedor my warm and grateful greetings - and a respectful salute for their courageous and great service at a critical time in the life of this nation.

Sincerely yours,

Harry Truman

Mr. Ralph M. Knox
8105 Overbrook Road
Leawood, Kansas

Congressman Lee H. Hamilton presented Ralph M. Knox the Prisoner of War Medal in a special ceremony at the U. S. Capitol in Washington, D.C., in 1986.

Chapter 35
Staying Connected

"Only connect!...
Live in fragments no longer."
Edward Morgan Forster

After living in Jasper, Indiana for quite a few years, I recently moved to Anderson, South Carolina to be near my sister Alice and her husband. Since arriving in Anderson, I've purchased my first computer and have been connected to the Internet. It's my intention to stay connected in the broader sense too. I'm going to continue to remind Americans of their government's desertion of its fighting men in the Philippines in 1941-42. Since World War II, we have fought two more wars in Korea and Vietnam in which our government only provided enough support to sustain the wars, but not to win them. This trend of limited or selected support was started by Roosevelt, Eisenhower, Marshall, and MacArthur in the early forties.

Even the Persian Gulf War of the early nineties

wasn't pursued to its logical conclusion, the defeat of the enemy, in this case Iraq. At least, not at the time of this writing.

The danger in all of this is that America's young men in the military have suffered before and may suffer again because of half-hearted support, a complete lack of support or downright deceit by our government and military leaders.

America's military men, and now women too, have historically been recruited or drafted from the less advantaged segments of the American population. This has been especially true since the sixties, when many men were able to avoid military service and the chance of being sent to Vietnam by becoming teachers or perpetual students, or by moving to Canada or Sweden. Many young teachers and students quit school after the war and danger of military service were over.

Unfortunately, President Bill Clinton was one of those well-educated youths who used his connections to avoid service. The worst part of it is that he lied to cover-up his selfishness. I wonder if Clinton is ever bothered by the chance that some young man from a city's ghetto might have been drafted to serve in Vietnam and died there in his place.

I was one of the disadvantaged when I enlisted back in 1940. I couldn't get a decent job. I couldn't earn enough to go to college. I joined the military, the only option really open to me back then. Mine could be the story of a young man from the sixties who was forced into the only job available to him—fighting for his country.

Our soldiers and airmen in the Vietnam War were deceived too. Promised help to win it, they never received the commitment and materiel to do the job. Their leaders, particularly Secretary of Defense Robert S. McNamara, knew we couldn't win but sacrificed the lives of thousands of American men anyway.

In his recent memoir, *In Retrospect: The Tragedy and Lessons of Vietnam*, McNamara complained that he and his family were harassed during the Vietnam War. Whatever harassment they suffered pales in comparison to the slaughter our armed forces personnel experienced in 1968 during Tet, for example.

McNamara used the domino theory to justify our sending troops to Vietnam. Supposedly, if one Asian nation fell to Communism, they would all collapse. The problem was that McNamara and his cronies couldn't tell the difference between a Communist uprising and a Nationalist movement, such as Ho Chi Minh's in Vietnam.

How does Robert McNamara live with himself today? I guess the same way Douglas MacArthur did, beginning March 17, 1942, in Australia.

The United States National Cemetery near Manila, the Philippines. This is the final resting place for 17,182 U. S. military dead. Most of those lost their lives in the defense of the Philippines and The Netherlands East Indies in 1941-42 or in the return of American forces, 1944-45. The cemetery site covers 152 acres and is the largest in area of the cemeteries built and administered by the American Battle Monuments Commission. It also has the largest number of graves and records concerning those missing. Names of the missing are listed on the walls of the cemetery's Memorial.

Chapter 36
Looking for Justice

"Recompense injury with justice,
and recompense kindness with kindness."
Confucius

"We want proper compensation, not joy trips for 80-year-old men out to Japan," said Arthur Titherington, chairman of the Japanese Labor Camp Survivors Association in Britain. Titherington was responding to a Japanese offer made in January 1998 to finance British veterans' visits to Asian battlefields and cemeteries. The Japanese also offered to pay for the grandchildren of British prisoners of war to study in Japan for a year.

Titherington could have been speaking for ex-POWs of the Japanese from many countries when he demanded proper compensation. Ex-POWs from the Philippines, Indonesia (former Netherlands East Indies), Korea, the Netherlands, Australia and the United States have all demanded to be compensated for their slave labor under the Japanese.

The Japanese offers to the British also included an

apology to Prime Minister Tony Blair for the suffering of British POWs in World War II. Ex-POWs in London said the apology didn't go far enough because it didn't include reasonable compensation. Many ex-POWs felt that the apology was extended only because Emperor Akihito, Hirohito's son, was to visit Britain in May 1998.

During that visit to London, Akihito was booed by hundreds of veterans and civilians, many wearing white sashes indicating their ex-POW status.

"Are they sorry? No, they're not really," said Estelle Cowley, one of the demonstrators in London. Pinned to her jacket was a tattered piece of cloth bearing the faded numbers 6/148. This was the number she was assigned as a Japanese POW at the age of 13.

"We had to wear this every day, parade in it, parade wearing it through snow or searing heat," the British missionary's daughter said of her days in a Japanese prison camp in China.

I certainly understand that woman's anger.

Throughout most of Southeast Asia, the Japanese treated the children in their POW camps no better than the soldiers, sailors, airmen, nurses, and civilians they had captured. In January 1944, for example, the Japanese removed all boys age 10 or over from their mothers' care and placed them in mens' camps in the Netherlands East Indies. Many of these boys had to perform coolie labor.

When Chris B. Droste, author of *Till Better Days*, found his 10-year-old son on Java after a month-long search at the end of the war, the boy was emaciated and working as a coolie slave. Droste had been a harbor pilot and was taken to Australia against his will on a ship carrying refugees to Australia in 1942. His wife, daughter and son were left behind to be herded into Japanese camps. It is bad enough to be a POW of the Japanese for 40 months let alone be free while your wife and children are POWs. Droste suffered from anxiety over his family's fate and guilt for being free himself.

Six days after Japan's surrender in August 1945, the Japanese cabinet met in the prime minister's residence to discuss what they believed to be "urgent measures." These urgent measures had nothing to do with the atomic bombings of two Japanese cities or the millions of homeless Japanese. Instead, the meeting was about how to satisfy American "sex-starved" occupying troops.

Fearing that the Americans would behave as badly as the Japanese had during the war, raping women and girls throughout its conquered empire, the Japanese government set up an organization to establish brothels for the Americans. The authorities then asked patriotic Japanese women to sacrifice themselves to American troops as "comfort women."

The Japanese had a lot of experience in establishing brothels of comfort women throughout its conquered territory. Korean, Filipino and Indonesian women of the Netherlands East Indies, as well as Dutch women from the Indies were forced into brothels as comfort women to serve Japanese soldiers. A Japanese general in China in the thirties, requested comfort women for his troops. The women duly arrived, listed as "war supplies."

As many as 200,000 teenage girls and women from throughout Asia were ordered to have sex with Japanese soldiers. They became victims of government sanctioned serial rape. For 47 years after the war, the Japanese government denied this brutal chapter of its wartime history.

In July 1992, the Japanese government reversed itself

and admitted that its military had recruited and organized tens of thousands of women in a vast network of government-run brothels during World War II. Prior to this admission, the government had maintained that these brothels, in which thousands of women died, were set up by entrepreneurs.

In 1994, the Japanese government announced it would solicit private contributions for a fund that would be used to compensate comfort women. Although some of the comfort women have accepted money from the fund, others demand that the Japanese government itself pay compensation.

As of August 1995, 72 women from South Korea, the Philippines, the Netherlands and China had sued the Japanese government for either an official apology or compensation as high as $22,000 or both. It would be impossible to corroborate the accounts by many women who say they were confined and repeatedly raped as sex slaves by Japanese troops.

"The Japanese Imperial Army," said one of the Filipino women, "did not give us any IDs." There is no physical evidence. Recollections of names and faces are vague.

There is no telling how many women throughout Southeast Asia were victimized as comfort women or sex slaves. The academic estimate of 200,000 for the total number of women forced into prostitution by the Japanese is reached by using formulas found in official Japanese documents that specify an ideal ratio of one comfort woman for every 40 or 50 Japanese soldiers.

Thus the total number of women enslaved as comfort women could be enormous. No relief organizations or rape-victim support groups were organized after World War II as there were 50 years later in Bosnia. The postwar International Military Tribunal did not take up the comfort women's cause, except for the cases of several Dutch victims. Only about 200-300 Dutch women were forced to be comfort women. The International Military Tribunal, by its lack of interest in the serial rape of hundreds of thousands of Asiatic women by Japanese troops, inflicted another injustice on those comfort women from Korea, the Philippines and China.

In late April 1998, a Tokyo court ruled that the Japanese government must compensate three South Korean women forced to be comfort women by the Japanese army. The ruling was the first in a lawsuit by former brothel victims, and awarded the women the equivalent of $2,300 each. In a surprisingly sharp ruling, the Japanese judge called the army's actions an example of sexual and ethnic discrimination and a "fundamental violation of human rights."

This ruling should have a profound effect on five other pending cases filed by former comfort women. It could encourage other sex slave victims to file similar lawsuits. I hope so.

The American Defenders of Bataan and Corregidor has joined with the Raoul Wallenberg Center for Civil Justice to correct another violation of human rights by the Japanese. In May 1998, I received a letter from the Raoul Wallenberg Center after it received my name along with other American POWs who were forced to do slave labor for private Japanese companies during the war. The letter states in part: "The Raoul Wallenberg Center for Civil Justice is committed to holding the Japanese companies accountable for the financial benefits they have reaped as a result of your labors." This sounded good to me, so I completed the forms and had them notarized and returned as required.

However, in November 1998, the Tokyo District Court rejected two separate compensation suits filed by ex POWs forced into slave labor by the Japanese army. The first ruling was a rejection of demands for compensation from seven plaintiffs on behalf of 20,000 ex-prisoners from Britain, the United States, Australia and New Zealand. A week later, the same Tokyo court rejected another compensation suit by eight former Dutch POWs who had also been forced into slave labor by the Japanese army. The Dutch plaintiffs sued for $176,000.

In both cases, the Tokyo court ruled that under international law, individuals in wartime compensation cases do not have the right to sue the government. The Japanese government maintains that the issue of compensation for POWs was resolved in 1951, when it signed the San Francisco peace treaty. But the Tokyo District Court, while rejecting both suits, did concede that Japan had committed human rights violations during World War II.

These rulings do not bode well for The Raoul Wallenberg Center for Civil Justice suit on our behalf.

An Associated Press September 8, 1951, article highlighting the terms of the 1951 Japanese Peace Treaty includes the following: "Japan agrees to indemnify Allied prisoners of war who suffered undue hardships; it waives all claims against the Allies arising out of the war." The treaty also says that differences over interpretation of the treaty not otherwise settled be referred to the International Court of Justice in The Hague.

In October 1998, the Japanese government apologized to South Koreans for its behavior during World War II in return for a vague absolution from the South Korean president visiting Tokyo. Then President Jiang Zemin of China arrived in November for the first visit ever by a Chinese head of state and asked for a similar apology. The Japanese prime minister expressed "deep remorse," but refused to apologize.

China is, of course, where the "Rape of Nanking" took place in the thirties. In that incident, 300,000 Chinese were brutally killed in Nanking by Japanese forces.

Not only are the Japanese refusing to recognize their responsibility for violating the human rights of millions of people in Southeast Asia, they are refighting World War II in paperback books published in Japan. Japan is winning the war in these books. The novels are pulp fiction, not serious literature. They are published only in Japanese and explore what might have happened if Japan had acted differently during the Pacific War. In one novel, for example, Japan captures Hawaii and makes it independent from the United States. In the same novel, Japan, armed with weapons more powerful than those it had during World War II, destroys the Panama Canal.

By avoiding responsibility for their actions, I'd say the Japanese are suffering from collective amnesia.

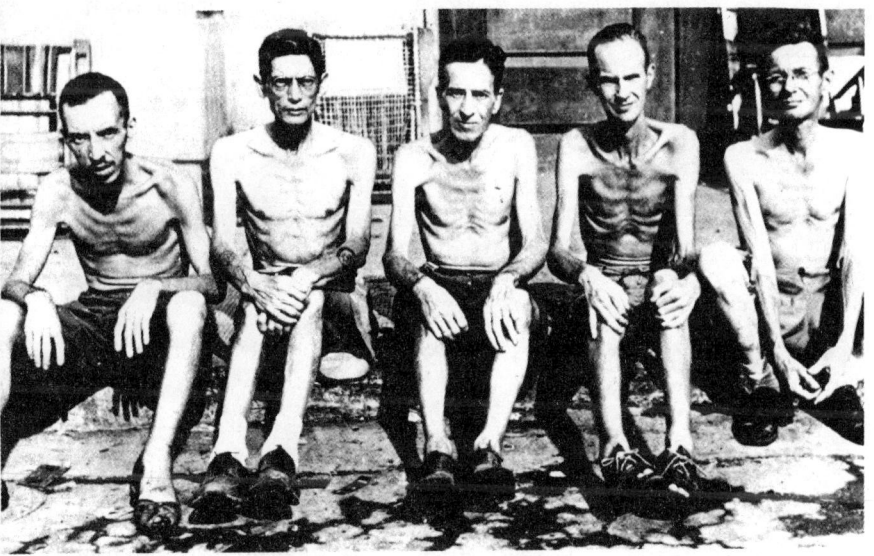

Five American ex-POWs of the Japanese photographed after Japan's surrender in August 1945.

(Left): Beheadings of Allied POWs by the Japanese were common throughout World War II. *(Bottom)*: An American POW of the Japanese assists another in a camp sick bay in Japan.

Chapter 37
Misplaced Justice

"...morale...will quickly wither and die if soldiers believe themselves the victims of indifference or injustice on the part of their government, or of...personal ambition or ineptitude on the part of their military leaders."

Douglas MacArthur, in the Annual Report of the Chief of Staff, U.S. Army, 1933

Though the Japanese have avoided apologizing for their actions and avoided compensating Allied ex-POWs for their slave labor in Japanese factories and camps, Public Law 100-383 was signed by President Ronald Reagan on August 10, 1988. Known as the Civil Liberties Act of 1988, the law stipulated that surviving Japanese-Americans who were relocated in internment camps after the 1941 bombing of Pearl Harbor by the Japanese receive reparations of $20,000 each.

Public Law 100-383 was unfair to the thousands of American ex-POWs of the Japanese whose chances of receiving compensation for their mistreatment are less likely as each day passes. The United States government has never addressed the issue that Japan must compensate American ex-POWs from the Pacific War. It leaves that problem to private organizations with much less clout, such as the Raoul Wallenberg Center for Civil Justice and the American Defenders of Bataan and Corregidor.

The United States ordered Latin American nations during the war to surrender 2,264 Latin Americans of Japanese descent for transport to the U. S. for internment. Surviving Japanese Latin Americans are now each entitled to $5,000 under the settlement of a lawsuit reached in June 1998. The settlement includes an acknowledgement of wrongdoing by our government and a letter from President Clinton to each of the plaintiffs in the class-action suit.

While the internment of Japanese-Americans in the early forties was an injustice to most of them, it does not compare to Japan's treatment of Allied POWs during the war!

When am I going to receive $20,000 and a letter of apology from the emperor? When will any American ex-POW of the Japanese receive a $5,000 or $20,000 compensation check? Probably never.

For the second time in our lives, we have been deserted by our own government.

Chapter 38
Whatever Happened to...

"If a man will begin with certainties,
he shall end in doubts;
but if he will be content to begin with
doubts he shall end in certainties."
Francis Bacon

After the war, I didn't have time to follow up on what had happened to the many officers and enlisted men that I knew from Clark Field and the war. Gradually, over the years, while doing my research, I learned more about the individuals I had known personally or who had a hand in my fate in the Far East from 1941-1945.

BULKELEY, Lieutenant John D., commander of the four patrol torpedo boats that took General Douglas MacArthur's party from Corregidor to Mindanao in March 1942: Led a fleet of 110 mine sweepers and torpedo boats at the vanguard of the Normandy D-Day invasion in June 1944. For his valor in battle, Bulkeley, who retired in 1988 as a Vice Admiral, was awarded the Navy Cross, two Silver Star

Medals, two Legion of Merit awards and the Purple Heart, in addition to the Medal of Honor he received for his exploits in the Philippines. His squadron's activities in the Philippines in early 1942 were chronicled in the book, *They Were Expendable*, by William H. White.

EUBANK, Col. Eugene, Commanding Officer of the 19th Bomb Group: Escaped to Java from the Philippines to carry on the war from there. His B-17s were based at a Dutch field at Malang on Java. In early March, after the Allied loss of the Battle of the Java Sea, the Japanese invaded Java from a large armada. Eubank piloted the last B-17 to escape Malang. After Eubank got in the air, the plane's occupants could see Zeros strafing the field below, setting a B-24 on fire. About 30 Americans left behind were captured and became Japanese POWs. Prior to World War II, Eubank had been an Army test pilot at the Air Corps experimental division at Dayton, Ohio. While at Dayton, Eubank became well-acquainted with Orville Wright, who expressed an interest in the work at the division.

MAITLAND, Lt. Col. Lester, former commanding officer of Clark Field: Escaped from The Philippines at midnight on December 24, 1941, in a Beech 18 with 5 other officers. The Beech 18, along with another one, had been originally assigned to fly young pursuit pilots to Australia. Instead, staff officers of the Far Eastern Air Force took their places. Maitland made it to Australia and was transferred to the European war. Later, he became an Episcopal minister.

SHIOZAWA, Corporal, the sadistic guard who beat my injured foot at Kawasaki: Known as "Little Dynamite,"

Shiozawa was given 20 years at Sugamo prison. General Douglas MacArthur, in another example of not looking out for his own, ordered Shiozawa's early release, along with other imprisoned guards, in 1958.

STASSEN, Commander Harold, who led Marines in Japan to free Allied POWs: Was elected Governor of Minnesota after the war and established the record for running for president more times than anyone. Stassen was on the USS *Missouri* as part of Admiral William F. Halsey's staff when an Army News Service release was read aloud to the admiral and his staff: "Through the Swiss government, Japan stated that she is willing to accept Potsdam terms provided the declaration does not compromise the prerogatives of the Emperor as sovereign ruler." Stassen immediately questioned the prerogatives of any sovereign ruler under an unconditional surrender. Admiral Halsey wanted to know if they had enough fuel to "hit the bastards once more before they quit."

WAINWRIGHT, Gen. Jonathan ("Skinny"), surrendered Corregidor to the Japanese in May 1942: He was liberated from Manchuria and flown to be an observer of the September 2, 1945, Japanese surrender ceremony on the USS *Missouri*. General MacArthur showed his prejudices again when approving the list of dignitaries to attend the surrender ceremony. MacArthur made certain that Wainwright and British Lieutenant General Arthur Percival were there. Percival had surrendered Singapore to the Japanese. MacArthur did not invite the Dutch officer who surrendered the East Indies to the Japanese, Lieutenant General Hein ter Poorten. All three officers had been held by the Japanese in Manchuria. Soon after the war, Wainwright was the guest of honor at Yakima, Washington's 1945 Armistice Day parade. Because the deserted hero was so frail, thin and elderly in appearance, the crowds fell silent in respect as he passed in an open car.

The only B-17 from Clark Field in December 1941 to survive World War II was eventually named *Swoose*, meaning a cross between a swan and a goose. It was basically a B-17D, but was fitted with enough parts scavenged from several other B-17s that had escaped to Australia to warrant the *Swoose* name. Captain Frank Kurtz was the pilot of the B-17 at Clark Field.

After the December 8, 1941, Japanese attack, he helped stack the dead Americans he had served with at Clark Field "like so much cord wood," he had later told his wife. After taking to the air to help defend Clark, he flew his B-17 first to Java and then to Australia. I probably made repairs on *Swoose* sometime or other while it was still at Clark Field. Swoosie Kurtz, the actress, is Kurtz's daughter and is probably the only actress named for an airplane.

Lieutenant General George H. Brett used *Swoose* as his personal plane when he was the deputy commander of Allied forces in Australia. *Swoose* is now in the possession of the Smithsonian Institution and is in storage awaiting restoration.

General Jonathan Wainwright on his way back to the U.S. after over three years as a POW of the Japanese. Major Gus Krause welcomes him at Hsian, China.

A Japanese poster celebrated the Japanese victories in 1942 over the U.S., Britain, China, and The Netherlands. The broken chain and letters ABCD symbolized Asia's freedom from the Americans, British, Chinese, and Dutch.

PART FOUR
APPENDICES

Appendix A
The United States at War

Official Report
By Gen. George C. Marshall
Chief of Staff, U.S. Army
Released at Washington
September 8, 1943

The following material has been exerpted from General Marshall's report. It provides the "official" version of events that led to the experiences of Ralph M. Knox in the Philippines. President Roosevelt called the overall report a "...fine, soldierly record of achievements...." in an effort to bolster the morale of the American people at home. The report does not mention the Bataan Death March, General MacArthur's indecision on December 8, 1941, or the details of General MacArthur's escape from the Philippines, using one B-17 just to remove the possessions of MacArthur's entourage, instead of carrying more Americans to safety.

Americans did not find out about the Bataan Death March until the Army and Navy made an unexpected joint announcement on the night of January 27, 1944. The announcement listed the following statistics: That 5,200 Americans from Bataan and Corregidor had died after the Death March; that 2,200 Americans had died at Camp O'Donnell in April and May 1942 and 3,000 more at Cabanatuan through October 1942.

These deaths were the first results of the actual record of achievement, as initiated by the actions of Roosevelt, Marshall, Eisenhower and MacArthur, from December 1941 through May 1942.

In July, 1941, the development of quantity production made it possible for the first time to assign modern materiel in sizeable lots to the Philippines. On August 28th the first flights of Flying Fortresses were started across the Pacific via Midway and Wake Islands and thence south through Rabaul, Port Moresby or Port Darwin, and north to the Philippines. By the first week in November some 35 Fortresses had completed this trip. A gap in airplane deliveries from the factory combined with adverse winds between San Francisco and Hawaii prevented the ferrying of an additional 48 Fortresses prior to the attack on Pearl Harbor.

July 26th General Douglas MacArthur was recalled from duty with the Philippine Commonwealth, placed on active duty, and designated as Commander of United States Army Forces in the Far East. Intimately familiar with the situation in the Philippines, he at once proceeded to expedite preparations for defense within the limits of the available munitions and trained manpower.

(...the Commanding General of the Philippines was directed to deliver gasoline and bombs to these points [Rabaul, Port Moresby, Port Darwin] and to Balikpapan in Borneo and Singapore in Malaysia. Deliveries to all but the last two points had been completed when the Japanese took the offensive, December 7th.)

National Guard antiaircraft and tank units which had progressed sufficiently in training and for which the necessary modern equipment could be provided were dispatched to the Philippines during this period of preparation. Some 100 light tanks and the first 50 self-propelled artillery weapons delivered by our arsenals were shipped to the Philippines and arrived prior to the outbreak of war.

In August, President Roosevelt issued a proclamation

mobilizing the Philippine National Army and steps were taken to furnish these partially trained forces with whatever equipment could be made available from the United States, in addition to that held in reserve in the Philippines. Referring to this mobilization of the Philippine forces and the shipments from the United States of troops, planes and other munitions already effected or in progress, General MacArthur in a letter to the Chief of Staff on August 30th made the following comment:

"I wish to express my personal appreciation for the splendid support that you and the entire War Department have given me along every line since the formation of this command. With such backing the development of a completely adequate defense force will be rapid."

In early September the War Department recommended to Congress that the Philippine Independence Act of 1934 be amended so as to authorize the expenditure of certain Sugar Excise Tax funds and currency devaluation funds accruing in the Treasury of the United States for defensive purposes in the Islands. These funds amounting to approximately $52,000,000 were wanted primarily for the extension of airfields. While awaiting legislative action the War Department obtained $10,000,000 from the Emergency Fund for the President to be utilized for Philippine defenses. This, plus another $10,000,000 from Army Air Force funds, was quickly exhausted and an additional $5,000,000 was obtained from the Emergency Fund for the President while the debate was in progress in Congress. Still later when the Sugar Excise Tax legislation did not receive favorable action the War Department included in the Third Supplemental National Defense Appropriation Act, 1942, $269,000,000 for the Army of the Philippines, but this did not become available until the

Act was approved on December 17, 1941.

By October, 1941, it had been found possible to assemble 500,000 tons of supplies and 20,000 fully equipped and fairly well trained troops as reinforcements for the Philippine Islands. Few troop transports were available, but with hasty conversion of passenger ships to troop carriers, 11 troop ships were scheduled to sail between November 21st and December 9th. Twelve cargo vessels were to sail between November 21st and January 6th. Six of the troop ships and nine cargo vessels were at sea when word of the Pearl Harbor attack was received. Orders were flashed to all of these vessels to proceed to the nearest friendly port and to observe radio silence. Four of the troop ships returned to San Francisco. The other two, which were well out from Honolulu with 4,500 troops aboard, made Brisbane, Australia, after 15 days of silence and uncertainty. All but one of the cargo vessels reached friendly ports. The exception was presumed captured after having reported on January 1st from 600 miles south of Tahiti that an unidentified airplane had ordered her to halt but that she was proceeding to New Zealand. Another vessel whose cargo included P-40 fighters, motor vehicles, rifles, ammunition,, and gasoline, was at Christmas Island at the time the Japanese struck. It immediately put to sea and no word was heard from it until the 23rd of December when it sailed into Los Angeles harbor with its cargo intact.

Further deliveries to the Far Eastern area were hampered by the loss of Wake Island which necessitated the immediate development of an alternate trans-Pacific route via Christmas Island, Canton Island, Fiji, and New Caledonia. The new route was opened to traffic during January 1942. In the interim all heavy bomber air movements were immediately undertaken from Miami, Florida, via Brazil, equatorial Africa, and India through Sumatra to Java and Australia. The loss of Sumatra in February terminated deliveries by this route. While this sudden reversal of a movement half way around the earth demonstrated the mobility of the airplane, it also demonstrated the lack of mobility of air forces until a lengthy process of building up ground service forces and supplies (mechanics, ordnance and radio technicians, signal personnel, radar warning detachments, antiaircraft, medical and quartermaster units, as well as the troops to capture airfields and defend them against land attack, and the accumulation of repair machinery, gasoline, bombs and ammunition) had been laboriously completed by transport plane, passenger and cargo ship—the last two largely being slow-moving means of transportation. The planes flew to Australia in 10 days. The ground units and materiel to service the planes and keep them flying required approximately two and a half months or longer for the transfer.

As an example of the degree of our shortages, the necessity for disapproving the requests of the Government of the Netherlands East Indies is cited. After urgent requests through the various channels the representatives of that government finally called on me personally in the latter part of August, 1941, and made a moving appeal for, among other things, an initial allotment of 25,000,000 rounds of small arms caliber .30 ammunition. They stated that they feared the disintegration of their ground forces unless at least a small amount of ammunition was promptly issued. We had an extremely critical situation here in the United States but the dilemma of these fine people was so tragic in the face of the Japanese threat that it was finally decided to accept the hazard of reducing the ammunition reserve for the troops in movement to Iceland to an extent which would permit seven million rounds being turned over to the Dutch. Four million of these rounds were to be made quickly available by shipment from Manila, replacement shipments being started from San Francisco immediately. (Incidentally, seven million rounds was to be the daily delivery of a plant which was due to get into production in early October, but that was to be too late for the gathering storm in the Far East.)

Our defense forces in the Philippines at the time of the Japanese attack on December 8, 1941 consisted of 19,000 United States Army troops, 12,000 Philippine Scouts and approximately 100,000 men of the newly mobilized and but partially trained and equipped Philippine Army. Included in these forces were some 8,000 Army Air Forces personnel equipped with some 250 aircraft, of which 35 were Flying Fortresses and 107 were P-40 fighters.

The enemy led off with systematic bombing of airfields and key points in Luzon which resulted in the destruction of a large number of our planes due to limited dispersal fields and lack of sufficient radar warning equipment, antiaircraft guns, and other materiel.

On December 10th and 22nd, Japanese landings were made in northwestern Luzon. Outnumbered and incompletely equipped, lacking air support, and utilizing troops but recently mobilized and organized for the first time into regimental groups, General MacArthur was left no alternative but that of a delaying action. His action was further complicated by another Japanese landing, in force, on the eastern coast of Luzon. Under great difficulties an orderly withdrawal was effected into the Bataan Peninsula for a final defensive stand, protected and supported by the fortress of Corregidor. The remaining bombing planes were sent to Mindanao (later to Australia) with the mission of securing bases from which to support the operations on Bataan. The enemy rapidly concentrated his forces ashore and launched heavy attacks against the Bataan garrison, which heroically contested every foot of ground.

(By the end of January, Japanese troops had seized the important oil center of Tarakan on the northeast coast of Borneo, captured Rabaul and Kavieng in the Bismarck Archipeligo and Kieta on Bougainville Island in the Solomons, were rapidly approaching Singapore from the north, and controlled the sea and air routes to the Philippines. They stood along a 4,000-mile frontier of the Dutch East Indies and the Melanesian Barrier with their forces in position to threaten the remaining Dutch possessions, Australia and the islands to its north and east.)

The difficulties of the supply situation on Bataan, under the Japanese blockade, were greatly aggravated by the fact that thousands of civilians accompanied the army onto the Bataan Peninsula. The number of people to be supplied quickly forced a reduction of the entire command to half rations. Efforts were immediately initiated to organize blockade running from the Netherlands East Indies and Australia and to carry medicines, special fuses, and other critical munitions by submarine. The blockade running, financed from the funds placed at the disposal of the Chief of Staff by Congress, involved many difficulties; for example, it was found that the small ship owners and crew members approached in Java, Timor, and New Guinea would not accept checks on our Federal funds deposited in Melbourne, but demanded cash. Therefore the actual money had to be flown across Africa and India by plane for delivery in Java. A complete report of these perilous operations has never been received. Of seven ships dispatched from Australia only three arrived at Cebu. Attempts to trans-ship these supplies from Cebu to Corregidor failed because of the rigid enemy blockade. At least 15 of these blockade runners, totaling 40,000 tons, were sunk or captured by the enemy while attempting to get supplies through to Bataan. Several over-age destroyers were also fitted out as blockade runners but none of these succeeded in reaching the Philippines prior to the fall of Corregidor.

The difficulty of penetrating the Japanese blockade and getting supplies to Corregidor and Bataan caused the military situation to deteriorate. The half rations issued since January 11, 1942, had been further reduced by the end of March, and horses and mules were being slaughtered for food.

In view of the enemy's capabilities throughout the Pacific and our untenable position in the Philippines, the major efforts of the United States were directed toward a rapid concentration of defense forces along our route to Australia, the creation of an effective striking force on that continent, and the dispatch of material aid to the forces of our Allies in the East Indies. Accordingly, Hawaii was strengthened, additional islands along the South Pacific air ferry route were garrisoned, and a large force was provided for the defense of New Caledonia. The components of a balanced air force were shipped to Australia, the heavy bombers being flown in via Hawaii or India. Shipping limitations precluded the early dispatch of large bodies of ground troops.

In February, 1942, General MacArthur was instructed by the War Department to proceed to Australia to assume command of the newly designated Southwest Pacific Area. His directive from the Combined Chiefs of Staff included the missions of holding Australia, checking the enemy's advance along the Melanesian Barrier, protecting land, sea and air communications with the Southwest Pacific and maintaining our position in the Philippines. Lieutenant General Jonathan M. Wainwright, succeeding General MacArthur as commander of the forces in the Philippine Islands, continued the gallant defense which has become an epic in American history.

On March 31st the Japanese initiated the anticipated general assault on the Bataan position, an attack relentlessly maintained during the next seven days. As our lines were finally penetrated and field hospitals were shelled by Japanese artillery, it became apparent that the courageous but exhausted defenders could no longer avoid disaster.

On April 9th the following radio message was received from General Wainwright on Corregidor:

"Shortly after the flag of truce passed through the front line this morning, hostilities ceased for the most part in Bataan. At about 10 o'clock this morning General King was sent for, to confer with the Japanese commander. He has not returned, as of 7 o'clock p.m., nor has result of conference been disclosed. Since the fall of Bataan the hostile air force has renewed its attack on Corregidor. This island was heavily bombed this afternoon but has suffered no damage of military consequence."

Despite Bataan's loss, Corregidor, Fort Drum, and Fort Hughes (all island fortifications) continued to resist enemy attacks with counter-battery and antiaircraft fire for nearly a month. On April 13th and 14th a squadron of American bombers from the south successfully attacked Japanese installations and shipping in the Philippine area.

On May 5th, after a week of intensive bombardment

which buried many of the shore defenses under landslides, the enemy made a landing on North Point of Corregidor. The shattered defenses were unable to dam the Japanese tide. The following day the exhausted and depleted forces were overwhelmed and finally surrendered.

The final spirit of General Wainwright's heroic command is indicated by the extract from a letter written by him just before Corregidor fell:

"As I write this we are subjected to terrific air and artillery bombardment and it is unreasonable to expect that we can hold out for long. We have done our best, both here and on Bataan, and although beaten we are still unashamed."

Appendix B
28th Bombardment Squadron, 19th Bombardment Group May 10, 1942 Roster

The following roster, though not necessarily complete as all personnel records were destroyed during the Japanese bombing of Clark Field, lists the men of the 28th Bombardment Squadron and their status as of May 10, 1942, the day of the U.S. Forces final surrender of the Philippines. A number of 28th personnel later died in Japanese prisoner of war camps and on Japanese hell ships en route to Japan. The roster was supplied by many sources and this version, updated by Southfarm Press editorial, is courtesy of Edward Jackfert, former commander of the American Defenders of Bataan & Corregidor, Inc.

KILLED IN ACTION, AS OF MAY 10, 1942
Corporal Joseph Hriczo   Private Darrel I. Edwards
Private Robert Jennings   Private Dhester Pokrzywa
Private Van Dyke

CAPTURED ON CORREGIDOR: ESCAPED
First Lieutenant Edgar Whitcomb

PRISONERS OF WAR: Second Lieutenants
H. Bryant   Basil H. Lewis
Robert D. Downes   William F. Lovegreen
Victor J. Howard   Charles L. Mathis
Robert D. Lanier   Joseph C. Milligan
Donald L. Larson   Roy D. Russell

PRISONERS OF WAR: Master Sergeants

Stanley A. Bowes
John W. Britton
Wilbur F. Disosway
Albert G. Kovel
Artie V. Lambert
Isadore Oricht
Westley H. Owens

PRISONER OF WAR: First Sergeant

J. Kristapoviz, Jr.

PRISONERS OF WAR: Tech Sergeants

Harold F. Beasley
Willie L. Gress
Harold J. Glass
Mike Sidas
Lloyd T. Leicester
Francis G. Lovelady
Andrew J. Oltz

PRISONERS OF WAR: Staff Sergeants

Reid Brock
Charles Daley
Auorey Freeman
Julle A. Hanson
Eugene L. Hartson
Watson J. Henley
William F. Hoy
Carl R. Jones
Ralph M. Knox
Paul E. Riddle
John Seres
William Tires
R. D. Sollenberger
Alfred R. Young

PRISONERS OF WAR: Sergeants

Paul Bellus
M. Birmingham
William A. DeRosa
Wiley L. Forrell
Frank R. Blaydes
Charles Callahan
Henry C. Lilly
Robert M. Call
Robert I. McCord
Henry J. Cornellisson
Clarence E. Ryley
Lee D. Stephens
John J. Furtado
Robert A. Hall
William A. Howard, Jr.

Roy L. Jobe
Edward A. Kozer
Donald J. McPherson
Donald A. Munn
Donald L. Naumann
Robert L. Renfro

Mike Tereletsky
John W. Weir
Ralph L. Westervelt
George S. Williamson
Dwight O. Woodall
Robert J. Endrees

PRISONERS OF WAR: Corporals

M. O. Algoe
George Wood
Ray Barger
Harold A. Bergbower
William P. Biggs
Marvin C. Buckem
Joseph C. Burke
Gordon Carnes
LeRoy Casey
Ben L. Creagle
William R. Diskauski
Jack C. English
William T. Frederick
Ralph E. Gottovi

Robert A. Jammer
Edwin E. Klan
Lawrence R. McGuire
Emory H. Pannell
Thomas B. Pierce
Oscar M. Powell
Bernard E. Prost
Keith W. Robertson
Curtis W. Schmeisser
Wayne M. Thompson
Elbert L. Van Cleave
Owen E. Wallisa
William H. Weaver

PRISONERS OF WAR: Privates First Class

Victor P. Adams
Robert D. Andalora
Robert T. Anderson
Charlie A. Antee
Max J. Arnold
Russell Arnold
Harold C. Bailey
Charles E. Bancroft

Thomas M. Bandy, Jr.
Edward A. Barber
Merlin N. Becker
Donald A. Bergum
Juillo E. Bodtker
James C. Bossinas
Clarence H. Brandt
Harold R. Brown

M. Browning
Robert P. Caudell
Aranda R. Callen
John O. Clayton
Kenneth M. Cobb
James Conroy
Charles H. Corneliuson
Robert E. Daken
Walter L. Daken
Harold D. Dalton
Frank H. Driver, Jr.
Paul E. Emerson
John W. Fox
John J. Gordon
Charles H. Graham
George E. Gresh
Robert C. Howren
Roy J. Hughes
Ernest J. Irving
Eddie Jackfert
Earl A. Kessler
Gillner Kittinger
Michael Kosakovitch
Marshall C. Leib
Oscar L. Leonard
Harold J. London
Richard Marlowe
James F. Hertens
Jack L. McKenzie
Michael L. Motich
Patrick D. O'Brien
Dalton D. Philips
Robert W. Philips
Ernest Poulin
Otis E. Radcliffe
Clyde F. Rasnake
Raymond R. Schauer
Lloyd R. Seifert
William J. Sheehan, Jr.
Edward B. Stapleton
Robert L. Stokes
James L. Sweeney
Willard W. Teibel
Frank W. Treida
Frank S. Watts
Norman E. Whitehead
Harold W. Wiley
Leonard W. Williams

PRISONERS OF WAR: Privates
Harry Baxter
Houston B. Buckner
Harold L. Copeland
Thomas E. Garity
Jack W. Grady
Eugene L. Hull
Edward C. Jensen
Sumner L. Kaplan
Joseph S. Loncz

Donald W. Mark
Irvin R. Reber
Robert H. Romy

Joseph R. Stanford
Chester S. Tomczuk
Charles E. Ward

PERSONNEL EVACUATED TO AUSTRALIA
BEFORE MAY 10, 1942 SURRENDER
Major William P. Fisher

First Lieutenants:
Thomas J. Christian
James T. Bruce
Thomas B. Hubbard

Dorwood C. Stephens
Ted B. Fisch

Second Lieutenants:
Hugh T. Halbert
William T. Chesser
Kenneth L. Culp
Everett Davis
Charles E. Rogers
James A. Hilton
Willis J. Gary
David M. Conley

Herbert F. Glover
Theodore Arter, III
Edward D. Benham
John W. Cox, Jr.
Peade R. Pickler
Lyle P. Thompson
Richard P. Haney
Lee C. Lester

Master Sergeants:
Jesse Gilbert
Louis W. Novak

Troy Stump
Thomas F. Toohey

Sergeants:
Joseph G. McElroy

Adolph E. Sternberg, Jr.

Corporals:
George W. Boss

James H. Holcomb

Private First Class:
Edward Lisiowski

Privates:
Jay C. Bailey
Frederick E. Freese

Wilbur W. Berry

FATES OF REMAINING PERSONNEL

M/Sgt. James P. McIntyre:	Missing May 10, 1942
M/Sgt. Peterson:	Stayed on Bataan
M/Sgt. Raymond Whitehead:	Left on Bataan
T/Sgt. Joseph Johnston:	Missing on flight December 12, 1941
T/Sgt. Carl H. Flodman:	Missing May 10, 1942
T/Sgt. Oliver R. Kamstra:	In hospital Dec. 8, 1941
T/Sgt. William T. Mason:	Left on Bataan
T/Sgt. John P. Wilson:	Left on Bataan
S/Sgt. Paul J. Brumley:	Left Philippines by air, December 15, 1941
S/Sgt. Robert E. Faust:	Missing May 10, 1942
S/Sgt. Jeffries	Unknown
S/Sgt. Frederick N. Murillo:	Accidently drowned in Pulangi River
S/Sgt. John Nagley:	OCS in U.S.
S/Sgt. Joseph D. Rose:	Left in hospital, Luzon
S/Sgt. Armande J. Viselli:	Missing on flight, December 12, 1941
Sgt. Frank R. Briggs:	Left on Bataan
Sgt. Durwood L. Brooks:	Missing May 10, 1942
Sgt. Joseph Halat:	Left on Bataan
Sgt. John J. Sheehan:	Left on Luzon
Sgt. Russell Smith:	Missing May 10, 1942
Cpl. Hubert E. Peacock:	Missing May 10, 1942
Pfc. Harlen A. Barrett:	Missing in action
Pfc. Everett R. Brooks:	Left on Bataan
Pvt. Toxie L. Coker:	Left on Bataan
Pvt. Robert E. Johnston:	Missing after SS *Mayon* Bombing
Pvt. James A. Mathieson:	Left on Bataan
Pvt. Pvt. Edison L. Powell:	Left on Bataan

The hospital ward for POWs of the Japanese in Bilibad Prison, Manila.

Appendix C
Principal Characteristics of Bombers: B-17, B-24, B-25, B-29, "Betty"

In the middle of the day on December 8, 1941, Colonel Eugene Eubank looked absently out the window from the Clark Air Field Headquarters building on Luzon, jumped back suddenly, and yelled out, "Take cover, men! Here they come!" "They" was the Japanese. Compare the principal characteristics of the B-17, our bomber on the ground, with "Betty," their bomber overhead, and the other important American bombers of the war.

B-24 Bomber

Appendix C□247

TYPE	DIMENSIONS	SPEED	BOMB LOAD	ARMAMENT	RANGE
B-17E* Long Range *B-17Cs and Ds were at Clark Field	Span: 103'9"; Length: 73'10"	317 mph at 25,000 ft. Cruise 195-273 mph	Max: 5,000 lbs. Normal: 4,000 lbs.	Thirteen 0.50 cal. Browning machine guns	3,300 mi. or 2,000 mi. with 4,000 bomb load
B-24D Long Range	Span: 110' Length: 99'	Max: 313 mph at 25,000 ft. Cruise: 233 mph	Max: 12,800 lbs. Normal: 5,000 lbs.	Ten 0.50 cal. Browning machine guns	Max: 3,600 mi. or 2,100 mi. with bomb load
B-25 Medium Range	Span: 67'7" Length: 51'	Max: 281 mph at 15,000 ft. Cruise: 248 mph	Max: 4,000 lbs. Normal: 3,000 lbs.	Thirteen 0.50 cal. Colt Browning machine guns	Max: 2,450 mi. or 1,560 mi. with 3,000 bomb load
B-29 Very Long Range	Span: 141.3'	Max: 358 mph at 30,000 ft. Cruise: 230 mph at 20,000 ft.	Max: 20,000 lbs. Normal: 10,000 lbs.	Twelve 0.50 cal. machine guns, one 20 mm cannon	Max: 5,600 mi. or 3,250 mi. with 20,000 lb bomb load
"Betty" Mitsubishi G4M Type I Heavy bomber	Span: 81'8" Length: 64'43/4"	Max: 292 mph at 15,000 ft. Cruise: 196 mph	2,000 lbs. or 1 large torpedo	Six 7.7 mm machine guns plus .20 mm tail cannon	Max: 2,671.9 mi.

Appendix D
Principal Characteristics of Pursuits: P-40 and "Zero"

To American pursuit pilots' amazement in the Philippines, Japanese "Zero" fighters were faster and more maneuverable than American planes and climbed at a terrifying rate. Americans had been told that there was no such thing as a good Japanese fighter plane. Over Clark Air Field in the Philippines, however, Americans learned the truth.

Exact data about the Zero had been sent to the War Department by General Claire Chennault in the fall of 1940. Chennault, as head of the Flying Tigers in China, also informed the War Department how the heavier P-40 could dominate the faster Zero. As Chennault wasn't very popular with Air Corps commanders, this information was filed away and not available to American pilots when the Zero appeared over the Philippines.

Appendix D 249

P-40 Warhawk fighter. It was the primary Army fighter at the outbreak of hostilities in the Philippines. It could outdive the Zero, but was outclassed otherwise.

TYPE	DIMENSIONS	SPEED	BOMB LOAD	ARMAMENT	RANGE
P-40K "Warhawk"	Span: 37'4" Length: 33'4" Height: 12'4"	Max: 362 mph at 15,000 ft. Cruise: 290 mph Climb: 15,000'/7.5 min.	500 lb. bomb	Six .50 cal. wing guns	Max: 1,600 mi. or 350 mi. with 500 lb. bomb
Zero Mitsubishi ("Zeke")	Span: 36'1" Length: 29' 8 3/4"	Max: 334 mph at 16,570 ft. Cruise: 207 mph Climb: 19,685'/7 min. 7 sec.	Two 66 lb. bombs	Two 7.7 mm machine guns, two 20 mm cannon	Max: 1,130 mi. at 152 mph, 875 mi. at 212 mph

Appendix E
Death Rates of Allied Prisoners of War in the Pacific: American, British, Australian, and Dutch

Japanese contempt for POWs was part of the basic training of Japanese soldiers. The Japanese believed it was cowardly to surrender to your enemy, that surrender brought dishonor to your family and family name. The Japanese troops did not distinguish between those who fought courageously and those who surrendered without fighting. To the Japanese, all POWs were the same. They all had lost their honor and were not entitled to any respect.

On Bataan, when the Americans surrendered in such large numbers, besides underestimating how many POWs would fall into their hands, the Japanese were surprised to receive requests from American commanders that they report the names of those captured to the U.S. government. The Japanese thought that those captured would not want their government and families to know of their dishonor.

Because of Japanese contempt for POWs of all nationalities, the death rate among POWs in the Pacific War was much higher than in the European War.

Appendix E 251

POWS OF THE JAPANESE
DEATH RATE BY NATIONALITIES:

American:

Total POWs:	Approximately 25,600
POW Deaths:	Approximately 10,650
Percentage Dead:	Approximately 41.6%

British, Australian, British Indian:

Total POWs:	Approximately 130,000
POW Deaths:	Approximately 8,100
Percentage Dead:	Approximately 6.2%

Dutch:

Total POWs:	Approximately 37,000
POW Deaths:	Approximately 8,500
Percentage Dead:	Approximately 23%

NOTE: As appalling as the above percentages of death among POWs were, none of them approached the percentages of death among the Asian forced laborers. The death rate of Indonesian forced laborers from The Netherlands East Indies was one of the worst examples.

Forced Laborers from The Netherlands East Indies (now Indonesia):

Laborers:	Approximately 300,000
Laborer Deaths:	Approximately 230,000
Percentage Dead:	Approximately 76.6%

In 1967, a scrapbook reminds Ralph Knox of his military service in the Philippines during World War II.

Bibliography and Sources

BOOKS

Bartsch, William H. *Doomed at the Start: American Pursuit Pilots in the Philippines, 1941-1942.* College Station: Texas A & M University Press, 1992.

Beck, John Jacob. *MacArthur and Wainwright: Sacrifice of the Philippines.* Albuquerque: University of New Mexico Press, 1974.

Boyington, Gregory "Pappy." *Baa Baa Black Sheep.* New York: Putnam, 1958.

Brereton, Lewis H. *The Brereton Diaries: The War in the Air in the Pacific, Middle East and Europe.* New York: William Morrow and Company, 1946.

Breuer, William B. *The Great Raid on Cabanatuan.* New York: John Wiley & Sons, Inc., 1994.

Carter, Kit C.; Mueller, Robert: compilers. *U.S. Army Air Forces in World War II, Combat Chronology: 1941-1945.* Washington, D.C.: Center for Air Force History, 1991.

Costello, John. *The Pacific War.* New York: Rawson, Wade Publishers, Inc., 1981.

Craven, Wesley Frank; Cate, James Lea: editors. *The Army Air Forces In World War II, Volume One: Plans and Early Operations, January 1939 to August 1942.* Washington, D.C.: New Imprint by the Office of Air Force History, 1983.

Daws, Gavan. *Prisoners of the Japanese.* New York: William Morrow and Company, Inc., 1994.

Dorf, Philip. *So Rich a Story: Highlights and Sidelights in American History.* New York: Oxford Book Co., 1969.

Droste, Chris B. *Till Better Days.* Middletown, Connecticut: Southfarm Press, 1992

Dower, John W. *War Without Mercy: Race & Power in the Pacific War.* New York: Pantheon Books, 1986

Dunn, William J. *Pacific Microphone.* College Station: Texas A & M University Press, 1988.

Eisenhower, Dwight D. *At Ease: Stories I Tell to Friends.* Garden City: Doubleday, 1967.

Friend, Theodore. *The Blue-Eyed Enemy: Japan Against the West in Java and Luzon, 1942-1945.* Princeton: Princeton University Press, 1988.

Fujita, Frank "Foo". *Foo: A Japanese-American Prisoner of the Rising Sun.* Denton, Texas: University of North Texas Press, 1993.

Gailey, Harry A. *The War in the Pacific.* Novato, CA: Presidio, 1995.

Goodwin, Michael J. *Shobun: A Forgotten War Crime in the Pacific.* Mechanicsburg, Pennsylvania: Stackpole Books, 1995.

Gunther, John. *The Riddle of MacArthur.* New York:

Harper & Brothers, 1951.

Heide, Sigrid. *In the Hands of My Enemy: One Woman's Story of World War II.* Middletown, Connecticut: Southfarm Press, 1996.

Hibbs, Ralph Emerson. *Tell MacArthur to Wait.* New York: Carlton Press, Inc., 1988.

James, D. Clayton. *The Years of MacArthur, Volume II: 1941-1945.* Boston: Houghton Mifflin Company, 1975.

Karig, Walter and Welbourn Kelley. *Battle Report: Pearl Harbor to Coral Sea.* New York: Farrar & Rinehart, Inc., 1944

Karnow, Stanley. *In Our Image: America's Empire in the Philippines.* New York: Random House, 1989.

Keith, Agnes Newton. *Three Came Home.* Boston: Little, Brown and Co., 1947.

Kelly, C. Brian. *Best Little Stories from World War II.* Charlottesville, Virginia: Montpelier Publishing, 1989.

Kerr, E. Bartlett. *Surrender & Survival, The Experience of American POWs in the Pacific 1941-1945.* New York: William Morrow and Company, 1985.

Ketchum, Richard M. *The Borrowed Years 1938-1941: America on the Way to War.* New York: Random House, 1989.

Lash, Joseph P. *Roosevelt and Churchill, 1939-1941.* New York: W.W. Norton & Co., Inc., 1976.

Leckie, Robert. *Delivered from Evil: The Saga of World War II.* New York: Harper & Row, 1987.

Lens, Sidney. *The Forging of the American Empire.* New York: Thomas Y. Crowell, 1971.

MacArthur, Douglas. *Reminiscences.* New York: McGraw

Hill, 1964.

Manchester, William. *American Caesar*. Boston: Little, Brown and Company, 1978.

Mason, John T. (Ed.). *The Pacific War Remembered*. Annapolis: Naval Institute Press, 1986.

McNamara, Robert S., Vandemark, Brian (Contributor). *In Retrospect: The Tragedy and Lessons of Vietnam*. New York: Vintage Press, 1996.

Messimer, Dwight R. *In the Hands of Fate*. Annapolis: Naval Institute Press, 1985.

Millett, Allan R., Murray, Williamson, Editors. *Military Effectiveness Volume III: The Second World War*. Boston: Unwin Hyman, 1988.

Mullin, J. Daniel. *Another Six-Hundred*. Mt. Pleasant, South Carolina: J. Daniel Mullin, 1984.

Parrish, Thomas. *Roosevelt and Marshall: Partners in Politics and War; The Personal Story*. New York: William Morrow and Company, Inc., 1989

Perret, Geoffrey. *Old Soldiers Never Die: The Life of Douglas MacArthur*. New York: Random House, 1996.

Russell of Liverpool, Lord. *The Knights of Bushido: The Shocking History of Japanese War Atrocities*. New York: Dutton, 1958.

Sayre, Francis B. *Glad Adventure*. New York: Macmillan Company, 1957

Snyder, Joe. *Para(graph) Trooper for MacArthur*. Leawood, KS: Leathers Publishing, 1997.

Stewart, Sidney. *Give Us This Day*. New York: W.W. Norton & Co., Inc., 1956.

Sunderman, James F. *World War II in the Air: The Pacific*. New York: Franklin Watts, Inc., 1962.

Thomas, David A. *The Battle of the Java Sea*. New York: Stein and Day, 1968.
Thorpe, Elliott R. *East Wind, Rain*. Boston: Gambit incorporated, 1969.
Toland, John. *But Not in Shame*. New York: Random House, 1961.
Vincent, Carl. *No Reason Why*. Stittsville, Ontario: Canada's Wings, Inc., 1981.
Waterford, Van. *Prisoners of the Japanese in World War II*. Jefferson, North Carolina: McFarland & Company, Inc., 1994.
Whitcomb, Edgar D. *Escape From Corregidor*. New York: Henry Regnery Co., 1967.
White, W. L. *They Were Expendable*. New York: Harcourt, Brace and Company, 1942.
Whitney, Courtney. *MacArthur: His Rendezvous with History*. New York: Alfred A. Knopf, 1956.
Willoughby, Major Gen. Charles A., Chamberlain, John. *MacArthur: 1941-1951*. New York: McGraw-Hill Book Company, Inc., 1954.
Wittner, Lawrence S. *MacArthur*. New Jersey: Prentice-Hall, Inc., 1971.

PERIODICALS
Author unknown. "Japan: Cold Comfort." *The Economist*, May 18, 1996, pp. 36-37.
Dyhouse, Tim. "Portraying the POW Experience." *VFW: Veterans of Foreign Wars Magazine*. September 1998, pp. 38-39.
Graves, William. "Corregidor Revisited," *National Geographic*, July 1986, pp. 118-131.
Lord, Mary. "Culture & Ideas: The Comfort Woman's

Cry," *U.S. News & World Report*, December 16, 1996, pp. 62-65.

Newbill, James G. "Brushes with History: The Cost of Courage,"*American Heritage*, May/June 1998.

Parshall, Gerald. "Special Report: The Strategists of War." *U.S. News & World Report*, March 16, 1998, pp. 50-79.

Porter, Russell. "Against Great Odds." *World War II Investigator* Magazine, October 1988, pp. 19-23.

Ramsey, Edwin Price, Rivele, Stephen J. "The Secret War of Ed Ramsey." *Reader's Digest*, March 1992, pp. 123-133, 185-212.

Taylor, Frank. "Battles Won & Lost: Agony in the Pacific," *American History*, June 1992, pp. 57-71.

Yoshihide, Soeya. "Viewpoints: Kim Seizes the Day." *Look Japan* Magazine, January 1999, p. 23.

PERSONAL ACCOUNTS

Sackett, E. L. "The *Canopus.*" This account was sent to families of POW's and MIA's of the Philippine defenders in March 1943. Sackett, Captain of the submarine tender USS *Canopus*, escaped Corregidor on May 4, 1942.

NEWSPAPERS

Associated Press. "China Angry at Japan Over WWII." *The New York Times On the Web*, November 27, 1998.

_____. "Japan Court Backs 3 Brothel Victims." *The New York Times On the Web*. April 28, 1998.

_____. "Japan Court Nixes Dutch POWs Suit." *The New York Times On the Web*, November 30,

1998.

———. "6 Phases of Jap Peace Pact Affect Wide Areas of Pacific. (Highlights of the Japanese Peace Treaty)." September 8, 1951.

———. "Tokyo Court Nixes WWII Compensation." *The New York Times On the Web*, November 27, 1998.

Author unknown. "'Comfort Women' Seek Justice From Japanese." *The Christian Science Monitor*, August 15, 1995, pp. 10-11.

———. "P.O.W. Ralph Knox Awarded Bronze Star After 40 Years." *The Butler* (Indiana) *Bulletin*, November 5, 1985, p. 1.

———. "World War II Prisoners of War Receive Contrast in Treatment." *The Ferdinand* (Indiana) *News*, November 10, 1988, p. 13.

Flint, Peter B. "General Minoru Genda, 84, Dies; Planned Attack on Pearl Harbor." *The New York Times*, August 17, 1989, p. B14.

Goldstein, Richard. "Sidney Stewart is Dead at 78; Bataan Death March Survivor." *The New York Times*, April 5, 1998, p. 40.

Knox, Ralph M. "Bataan Anniversary Recalls Bitter Days in Philippines." *The Kansas City* (Missouri) *Star*, May 7, 1967, p. 1F.

Kristof, Nicholas D. "Japan to Pay Women Forced Into Brothels." *The New York Times*. June 15, 1995, p. A10.

———. "Kokura, Japan: The City the A-Bomb Passed Over." *The New York Times*, August 7, 1995, p. A7.

———. "Fearing G.I. Occupiers, Japan Urged Women

Into Brothels." *The New York Times*, October 26, 1995, p. A1.

MacGregor, Hilary E., *Los Angeles Times*. "Fund for 'Comfort Women' Coming Up Short in Japan." *The Hartford Courant*, December 31, 1995, p. A13.

Passell, Peter. "Economic Scene: Make War, Not Money." *The New York Times*, May 23, 1990, p. D2.

Payne, Murray. "Jim McClelland Recalls Long Period as Prisoner of War." *The Tifton* (Indiana) *Gazette Family Weekend*, June 20, 1987, p. 1.

Pollack, Andrew. "Japanese Refight the War, and Win, in Pulp Fiction." *The New York Times*, March 4, 1995, p. 1.

Sanger, David E. "Japan Admits It Ran Army Brothels During War." *The New York Times*, July 7, 1992, p. A1.

Swarns, Rachel L. "Vice Adm. John D. Bulkeley, 84, Hero of D-Day and Philippines." *The New York Times*, April 8, 1996.

Thomas, Jr., Robert McG. "Frank Kurtz, 85, World War II Hero, Dies." *The New York Times*, November 9, 1996, p. 52.

Thomas, William, Scripps Howard News Service. "POW Story Helps Explain Why Thousands Still Resent Japan." *The Evansville* (Indiana) *Courier*, January 14, 1992, p. C7.

Treon, Ed. "Shock of Pearl Harbor, Bataan Horrors Recalled." *Fort Wayne* (Indiana) *News-Sentinel*, December 7, 1971, p. 1D.

Index

A-24s, 36
Abraham Crijnssen (minesweeper), 99
Act of Havana, 33
Africa, 233, 235-36
Akers, Anthony, Ensign, 93, 98
Akihito, Emperor, 212
Akin, Spencer B., Brigadier General, 95
Akita, 170
Ala Maru (Hell Ship), 133
Alanib, 122
Alaska, 24
Allies, 33, 63, 64, 76, 138, 164, 170, 236
Allied Fleet, 99
Allied prisoners, 133, 137, 144, 150, 159, 161, 177, 223
Altar of Freedom, 202
American Caesar (book), 96
American Defenders of Bataan and Corregidor, 199, 202, 215, 220

American Legion, 192, 204
Anderson, South Carolina, 207
Angeles, 29, 30, 40
Angrist, Joshua, 196
Aparri, 48, 49, 50
Arizona, USS (battleship), 43
Army Air Corps, 21
Arnold, Hap, General, 62, 109, 163
Ashigari (cruiser), 68
Asiatic Fleet, 99
Associated Press, 216
At Ease (book), 61
Atterbury, Camp, 185, 188
Atlantic Charter, 34
Australia, 63, 67, 69, 70, 71, 77, 81-2, 92, 94, 97, 98, 99, 101, 102, 103, 106, 113, 124-25, 149, 159, 202, 212, 216, 222, 224, 232, 233

262 Index

Award (Bronze Star), 204
Axis Powers, 37, 42, 76

B-10A, 28, 31
B-17s, 31, 32, 36, 39, 43, 44-5,
    48, 50, 53, 67, 68, 69,
    77, 94, 95, 96, 97, 164
    204, 222, 224, 246-47
B-25s, 109-10, 111, 114, 246-47
B-29s, 163, 167, 168, 170, 173,
    246-47
Baguio, 50, 70
Balikpapen, Borneo, 151
Bandung, Java, 138
Bansalan, 88
Bataan, 11, 42, 63, 65, 71, 72
    80, 81, 93, 97, 99, 102,
    103, 104, 113, 114, 117,
    125, 200, 202, 234, 235-36
    237-38; announcement of
    fall, 104-06, 113, 118;
    death march, 106, 130, 191,
    202, 229
Batan Island, 49
Batavia (now Jakarta), 150
Batchelor Field, 69
Beahan, Kermit, 167
Beebe, Lewis, Brigadier General, 118
Beech 18, 222
Belgium, 24, 33
Bell, Don, 50
Bellus, Paul, Sergeant, 58, 71,
    72, 80-1, 86-7, 240
Benevolence, USS (hospital
    ship), 174, 176
Berhala Island, 106

Blair, Tony, Prime Minister,
    212
Blocker, Colonel, 186, 188
Bombs, plutonium, 167;
    uranium, 167
Bonefish, USS (submarine), 137
Borneo, 92, 106, 147, 148,
    151, 230, 235
Bouganville Island, 235
Boyington, Gregory "Pappy,"
    Colonel, 174
Brazil, 232
Brazil Maru (Hell Ship), 137
Breck Shampoo ads, 189
Brereton, Lewis H., Major
    General, 35, 36, 39
    44-5, 48, 49, 62, 63,
    70, 71, 77, 114
Brett, George H., Lieutenant
    General, 224
Brisbane, Australia, 232
Britain, 31, 33, 76, 92, 159,
    169, 211. 212, 218
British, 63, 64, 92, 114, 141,
    149, 159, 211; Fleet,
    124
Bronze Star, 204
Brooklyn Navy Yard, 24
Bugo, Mindanao, 84
Bulkeley, John D., Lieutenant,
    93, 98, 221-22
Burma-Siam Railway, 149
Butler, Indiana, 20, 23, 142,
    186-88
Burma, 137

Cabanatuan, 103, 130, 134,

148, 229
Cabcaben, Bataan, 72, 118
Cagayan, Mindanao, 133
California, USS (battleship), 43
Call, Robert M., 28, 54
Callahan, Charles, Sergeant, 143, 156
Canada, 64, 208
Canangay, 151
Canberra, 124
Canton Island, 232
Caribbean, 34
Canopus, USS (tender), 54
Carmen Ferry, 85, 86, 87, 113, 121
Casey, Hugh J., Brigadier General, 95
Cavite Naval Base, 26, 27, 54, 67, 73, 79
Cawley, Frank, 193
Cebu, 27, 98, 236
Celebes, 92
Chanute Field, 23, 54
Chennault, Claire, General, 24, 248
Chicago, 201
China, 35, 44, 110, 143, 192, 193, 212, 214, 217, 248
China Clipper, 30
Chineses amah, 93, 95, 96
Chosen, 136
Christmas Island, 232
Churchill, Winston, Prime Minister, 31, 33-7, 44, 47, 61, 64, 76, 77, 92, 194
Chynoweth, Bradford G., Brigadier General, 101
Clark Field, 11, 17-8, 27-32, 39, 40, 42, 45, 47-55, 57-9, 63, 67, 68, 70, 71, 72, 94, 134, 143, 148, 184, 202, 224
Cleave, Harold L., Commander, 159, 160
Clinton, Bill, President, 208
Columbus, Indiana, 185
Communism, 209
"Comfort Women," 213-15
Congress, U.S., 64
Coral Sea, Battle of, 111
Corregidor Island, 11, 26, 27, 63, 65, 72, 73, 80, 84, 93, 97, 99, 101, 103, 104, 111, 113, 114, 117, 118, 122, 123, 134, 200, 201, 202, 235-36, 237-38
Costa Rica, 64
Cowley, Estelle, 214
Cuyo Islands, 93
Czechoslovakia, 24

Daly, M. F., Major, 81
DC-3, 185
Darwin, 69, 77, 94, 230
Davao, Mindanao, 51; Penal Colony, 148, 150
Davao-Digos Front, 85, 86, 88, 113
Dayton, Ohio, 191, 222
D-Day, 222
Death March, Bataan, 11
Del Carmen, Mindanao, 51, 67
Del Monte Field, 39, 67, 68, 69, 70, 93, 94, 95, 97, 113

Denmark, 24, 33
Diller, LeGrand A., Lieutenant Colonel, 95
Dole Pineapple, 26
Doolittle, James H., Lieutenant Colonel, 109-10, 142
Dove, Mr., 185
Dovey's Diner, 185
Droste, Chris B., 212-13
Drum, Fort, 239
Dutch, 63, 65, 92, 99, 114, 124, 138, 148, 149, 150, 151, 213-14, 222, 223, 234, 235
Dutch East Indies, see Netherlands East Indies

East Indies, 63, 65, 92
East Wind, Rain, (book and code), 41, 42
Eisenhower, Dwight D., Lieutenant Colonel, 61, 62, 65, 77, 99, 207, 229
England, 34
Endrees, Robert J., Sergeant, 88-9, 242
Enola Gay (B-29), 167
Enoura Maru (Hell Ship), 137
Enterprise, USS (aircraft carrier), 110
Escape from Corregidor (book), 202
Eubank, Eugene, Colonel, 31, 48, 50, 52, 70, 94, 114, 222, 246, 248
Europe, 24, 33, 34, 40, 61, 65
Europeans, 149
"Europe First Policy," 190
Ex-POWs, 177, 211-12

Far East Air Force, 35, 53, 69, 70, 75, 222
"Fat Man," 167
FEAF, 35, 53, 69, 70, 75, 222
5th Air Base Squadron, 11
Fiji, 232
Filipino Scouts, 152
Filipino troops, 77
Fischer, Harold "Red," First Lieutenant, 28, 48, 49, 68
Florida, 109, 232
"flying coffin," 28
Flying Fortress (B-17s), 39, 230, 234, 246-47
Flying Tigers, 25, 188, 248
Ford Island, Pearl Harbor, 43
Formosa (Taiwan), 39, 42, 44-5, 48, 49, 50, 62, 135, 137
Fort Wayne, Indiana, 193
14th Bombardment Group, 81
Fox, Bill, 161
France, 24, 33
French Indochina, 35
Funk, General, 103

Gaboli, Primitiva, 80, 82
Galletti, George, 160-61
Genda, Menoru, General, 194-95
Geneva Convention, 104, 133-34, 135
George, Harold, General, 70, 95, 114
German U-boats, 35
Germany, 33, 37, 63, 64, 76, 77

Gillie, Congressman, 189
Give Us This Day (book), 138
Gonzaga, 68
Goode, Coach, 21
Gottlieb, Leonard, 159
Greater East Asia Co-Prosperity Sphere, 147
Greer, USS (destroyer), 34
Guadalcanal, 111
Guam, 25, 36, 45, 110, 150, 179

Halsey, William F., 110, 223
Hall, Lieutenant (j.g.), 150
Hamilton, Lee H., Congressman, 9, 204
Haruna (battleship), 68
Harvard University, 199
Hawaii, 25, 31, 35, 41, 42, 43, 44, 45, 61, 236
Heide, Sigrid, 187
Helfrich, C. E. L., Vice Admiral, 63, 92
Hell Ships, 133-38, 163, 203
Hickam Field, 43
Hickey, John, 204
Hirohito, Emperor, 169, 175-76, 212
Hiroshima, 167, 177
Hitler, Adolf, 24, 33, 34, 40, 76, 196
Ho Chi Minh, 209
Homma, Masaharu, General, 118
"honey dippers," 145
Hong Kong, 45, 63, 76, 141, 147, 159, 161, 202
Honolulu, 25, 26, 232
Honshu, 136
Hornet, USS (aircraft carrier), 110

Houston, USS (cruiser), 70, 99
Houston Chronicle, The, 167-68
Huff, Sidney L., Lieutenant Colonel, 95, 96
Hughes, Fort, 237
Hull, Cordell, 35, 44
Hurt, Marshall H., Major, 104

Iba, 48, 49, 51, 53, 63
Iceland, 34
Illinois, 23, 185
Independence, Missouri, 199, 200
India, 233, 235-36
Indiana, 204, 206, 209
Indianapolis, Indiana, 21, 161
Indianapolis Indians, 21
Indianapolis Star, 161
Indonesia, 57, 211
In Retrospect: The Tragedy and Lessons of Vietnam (book), 209
Interceptor Command, 70
International Court of Justice in The Hague, 216
International Date Line, 17, 47
International Military Tribunal, 214, 215
In the Hands of My Enemy (book), 187
Iraq, 208
Italy, 61

Jackfert, Edward, 11, 28, 242
Jakarta (Batavia), Indonesia, 150
Japanese flag, 17, 51, 134
Japanese Imperial Navy, 42, 68, 80, 111

Japanese invasion (of the Philippines), 64, 69, 70, 77, 79, 113, 118
Japanese Labor Camp Survivors Association, 211
Japanese language, 129-30, 142, 157
Japanese reconnaissance planes, 40
Japanese surrender, 173-77, 213, 223
Japanese task force, 49, 50-1
Jasper, Indiana, 204, 207
Java, 41, 63, 70, 71, 137, 138, 149, 150, 212, 222, 224, 233, 235-36
Java Sea, 99, 150; Battle of, 222
Jeffries, Staff Sergeant, 32
Jenkins, Cletis, Coach, 20
Jerome, Jennie, 77
Jolo Islands, 51
Junyo Maru (Hell Ship), 137

Kai Tak Airfield, 45
Kalatungan Mountains, 122
Kanamuri, First Lieutenant, 150
Kansas City, 194
Kavieng, 235
Kawasaki Prison Camp, 13, 141, 222
Kawasaki War Dispatch Number 5, 141
Kearny, USS (destroyer), 35
Kelly, Colin P., Captain, 67
Kelly, Robert, Lieutenant, 93, 98
Kentucky, 189
Kerr, E. Bartlett, 152

Keschner, Harold W., 159, 160
Kieta, 235
Kimmel, Husband E., Admiral, 35, 43
King, Edward P., Major General, 102, 103-04, 118, 237
Kitakyushu, 167
Knox family: Alice, 14, 21, 204, 207; Evelyn, 21; Charles, 21, 188; James, 21, 188-89; parents, 19-22, 30, 192-93; Robert, 19, 188
Knox, Ralph M.:
  After war: 185-90, 192-94;
  Discharged from Army, 191
  Early years, 19-22
  Electronics company, 194, 2
  Employment after war, 193
  Hospitalized, 155-57, 179-8 191
  Injured, 155-57
  Meeting with Harry Truma 199-201
  Military decorations, 180, 2
  Military enlistment, 21-2
  Military, pre World War II, 23-6
  Prisoner of war, 129-170, 2
  Rescued, 173-77
  Sat for artist, 189
Kodama, Hideo, Baron, 148
Korea, 136, 148, 207, 211, 213, 214
Kokura, 167
Kowloon, Hong Kong, 202
Koyanaji, H., 161

Index □ 267

Kristopolis, First Sergeant, 28 240
Krueger, Alan, 196
Kurtz, Frank, Captain, 224
Kurtz, Swoosie (actress), 224
Kurusu, Saburo, 35
Kyushu, 110, 167

Lake Lanao, Mindanao, 121, 122
Lamao, 104
Lange, Eugene, 28
Legaspi, 51, 69
Lend-Lease, 34, 65
Letterman General Hospital, 179-81
Lewis, Hanna, 189
Lexington, USS (aircraft carrier), 37
Lieb, Marshall, 28, 242
Life Magazine, 201
"Little Boy," 167
Lopez, Salvador, 104
LST 1038, 176
Lugar, Richard G., Senator, 9
Luneta grandstand, 201
Luzon Island, 67, 72, 80, 101, 102, 130, 134, 148, 150, 234

MacArthur, Arthur, 93, 95, 96, 97, 115, 125
MacArthur, Douglas, General, 35, 36, 39, 42, 44, 48, 49, 50, 61-5, 69, 70, 75, 77, 79, 80, 92, 93, 95, 96, 97, 98, 99, 101-06, 113, 114, 115, 121, 124-25, 180-81, 186 192, 194, 202, 204, 207, 223, 229, 230, 231, 234

MacArthur, Jean, 95, 96, 97 115, 125
MacArthur's personal belongings, 96, 97, 125
Maitland, Lester J., Lieutenant Colonel, 31, 114, 222
"Maitland's Folly," 32
Malaya, 41. 92, 114, 124, 137, 150
Malay Archipelago, 99
Malaybalay, Mindanao, 85, 88, 122, 123
Malinta Tunnel, 80, 117-18
Manchester, William (historian), 96
Manchuria, 223
Manila, 35, 42, 50, 61, 62, 67, 69, 72, 75, 77, 79, 80, 96, 119, 134, 202, 203, 204
Manila Bay, 25, 67, 72, 83, 84, 96, 117, 134
Mao Tse-Tung, 202
Maramag, Mindanao, 121, 122
Marcos, Ferdinand, President, 200, 201, 202
Marcos, Imelda, 202
Margot River, Mindanao, 58
Marianas Islands, 170
Mariveles, Bataan, 72, 84
Marquat, William F., Brigadier General, 95
Marshall, George, C., General, 36, 44, 61, 62, 65, 77, 96, 103, 125, 207, 229-38
Marshall Islands, 45
Marshall, Richard, General, 95
Martin, "Shorty," 28, 47
Maryland, USS (battleship), 43

Matoba, Major, 150
Maxon, C. J. (car dealer), 21, 192
Mayon, SS (inter-island steamer), 83-4
McKinley, Fort, 27, 70
McMicking, Joseph, Captain, 95
McNamara, Robert S., 208-09
Melanesian Barrier, 235, 237
Melbourne, 235
Miami, 232
Midway Island, 111
Mindanao, 67, 68, 70, 84, 85-9, 93-5, 98, 101, 111, 113, 114, 122, 130, 137, 235
Mindoro, 84
Missouri, 194, 199, 200
Missouri, USS, 174, 175, 176, 223
Mitsubishi Motor Corp., 195
Mitsubishi Steel Mill, 141
Minnesota, 223
Moji, 136, 141
Monroe Doctrine Defense, 33
Moore, George, General, 101
Morhouse, Charles H., Major, 95
Moros, 57, 85, 86
Moulmein, 137
Mukden, Manchuria, 223

Nagano, General, 104
Nagasaki, 167, 177
Nagato Maru (Hell Ship), 148
Nanking, China, 217
National Bureau of Economic Research, 196
National Guard, 34, 230
Naval Control Center, 43
Navy, U. S., 34
Nazis, 24

Negros Island, 84
Neilson Field, 48, 67, 148
Netherlands East Indies, 41, 57, 64, 99, 149, 159, 211, 212, 233, 235
Netherlands, the, 24, 33, 169, 211
Neutrality Act, 34-5
Nevada, USS (battleship), 43
New Caledonia, 232, 236
Newfoundland, 34
New Guinea, 99, 169, 235
Newport, Kentucky, 189
New York, 24, 77, 159
New Zealand, 216, 232
Nicaragua, 64
Nichols Field, 27, 51, 54, 67, 148
Nineteen-Fortitude, 84
19th Bombardment Group, 31, 70, 239-44
Nippon Oil Refineries, 170
Nippon Steel Camp, 156-58
Nippon Steel Hospital, 156
Nitimei Maru (Hell Ship), 137
Nomura, Kichisaburo, 35
Normandy, France, 221
Norway, 24, 33
Nowels, Mildred (Aunt), 144
Nowels, Robert Earl (Uncle), 176

Oberlin, Joe, 193
O'Donnell, Camp, 130, 229
Ohio, 193, 195
Oklahoma, USS (battleship), 43
Op ten Noort (hospital ship), 150
Ord, James, 62
Oryoku Maru (Hell Ship), 137
Osaka, Japan, 148

Index

P-40s (pursuits), 36, 51, 53, 69, 70, 122, 232, 234, 248-49
P-35s (pursuits), 69
Pacific Fleet, 35, 43
Pacific War, 9, 10, 11, 14, 36, 42, 99, 111, 164, 169
Palawan Airfield, 148
Panama Canal, 24, 217
Pan-American Pact, 33
Pearl Harbor, 17, 35, 41, 42, 43, 44, 47, 50, 62, 76, 109, 195, 230, 232
Penang, Malaya, 137
Penguin, USS (Guam station ship), 45
Pennsylvania, 159
Percival, Arthur, Lieutenant General, 223
Perry, Andy, 193
Persian Gulf War, 207-08
Philadelphia, 200
Philippines Herald, The, 76, 79
Philippine Islands, 10-11, 24-26, 27, 31, 35, 36, 39, 41, 42, 43, 44, 49, 61, 62, 67, 69, 70, 75, 77, 91, 93, 94, 98, 99, 101-02, 114, 148; Fall of, 101-09, 117-19
Piang (Moro Chieftan), 85
Pinatubo, Mount, 17, 30, 51
Poland, 24
Port Moresby, 230
President Pierce, SS, 25, 26, 27
Prince of Wales, HMS, 34, 124
Princeton University, 196
Prisoners of the Japanese in World War II (book), 138

Prisoner-of-war camps, 11, 13, 123, 141-45, 147-52, 155-57, 163, 167-8, 173; hell ships, 133-38; medal, 206; mines, 13; railroad construction projects, 13, 149; steel mills, 13, 141-45, 155-57
PT-41, 93, 98
PT-34, 93
PT-35, 93, 98
PT-32, 93, 98
Pusan, Korea, 136

Quezon, Manuel, President, 62, 91

Rabaul, 230, 235
Rantoul, Illinois, 23
Raoul Wallenberg Center for Civil Justice, 215, 220
"Rape of Nanking," 217
Ray, Harold G., Captain, 95
Red Cross, 135, 137, 144, 159, 161, 176-77
Repulse, HMS (battle cruiser), 124
Reuben James, USS (destroyer), 35
Reyes, Norman, 104
Rockwell, Francis, Rear Admiral, 93, 95
Rogers, Paul P., Master Sergeant, 95
Roi, Marshall Islands, 45
rookies, 203
"Rookies on Parade" (movie), 203
Roosevelt, Franklin D., President, 23-4, 31, 33-7, 42, 44, 47, 61, 64, 76, 91-2, 99, 102, 103, 109, 110, 125, 187, 192, 194, 207, 229, 230-31

270 □ Index

Roosevelt, Theodore "Teddy," President, 27
Roudebush, Richard, Congressman, 204
Russia, 170

Sackett, E. L., Captain, 54-5
Saipan, 170
Salvation Army, 177
Samat, Mount, 202
San Fernando, 49, 50
San Francisco, 25, 26, 31, 110, 179-80, 185, 216, 232
Sayre, Francis B., 114, 203
Schumacher, V. S., Lieutenant (j.g.), 93, 98
Selfridge Field, 24
17th Pursuit Squadron, 51
Shanghai, 44
Sharp, William F., Brigadier General, 87-8, 93, 94, 101, 121-23
Sheridan, Fort, 191
Sherr, Joe R., Lieutenant Colonel, 95
Shigemitsu, Mamoru, 175
Shinagawa Hospital, 156, 159-61, 174, 188, 189, 200
Shinyo Maru (Hell Ship), 137
Shiozawa, Corporal, 157, 194, 222
Short, Walter, Lieutenant General, 35
Silver Star, 89
Singapore, 45, 64, 92, 223, 230, 235
Skymaster, 179

Slave labor, 211, 212, 215-16
Smith, Captain, 159
Smithsonian Institution, 224
Solomon Islands, 111, 235
Songer, Hugo C., Judge, 10
South Carolina, 207
South China Sea, 26, 51, 84, 117
Stark, Harold, Admiral, 44
Stassen, Harold, Commander, 173-74, 200, 223
Stewart, Sidney, 138
Stimson, Henry L., Secretary of War, 44, 77, 92
Stivers, Charles P., Colonel, 95
Stotsenburg, Fort, 28, 29, 52, 53, 58, 59, 71, 102-3
Subic Bay, 27
Suez Maru (Hell Ship), 137
Sugar Excise Tax funds, 231
Sumatra, 99, 150, 170, 233
Surrender and Survival: The Experience of American POWs in the Pacific 1941-1945 (book), 152
Sutherland, Richard, Major General, 36, 93
Suzuki, Colonel, 142, 194
Sweden, 208
Sweeney, Charles, Major, 167
Swoose (B-17), 224

Tacoma, Washington, 58
Tahiti, 232
Taiwan (Formosa), 135
Takao, 137
Task Force Mike, 110
Tatara (gunboat), 44

Tennessee, USS (battleship), 43
ter Poorten, Hein, Major General, 41, 138, 223
Thailand, 41
They Were Expendable (book), 222
3rd Pursuit Squadron, 51, 53
Third Supplemental National Defense Appropriation Act, 1942, 231
30th Bombardment Group, 81
34th Pursuit Squadron, 51
"thirty seconds over Tokyo," 110
Thorpe, Elliott R., Brigadier General, 41, 42
Tibbets, Paul, Colonel, 167
Till Better Days (book), 212
Tjideng Camp (Batavia), 150
Timor, 235
Tinian, 167
Titherington, Arthur, 211
Tojo, Hideki, General, 148, 176, 195
Tojo, Katsu, 195
Tojo, Teruo, 195
Tokyo, 13, 42, 109-10, 114, 141, 149, 163, 164, 170, 174, 195, 215, 216
Tottori Maru (Hell Ship), 134-37
Tradewind, HMS (submarine), 137
Trout, USS (submarine), 96, 111
Truman, Harry S, President, 188, 199-201
28th Bombardment Squadron, 11, 28, 31, 72, 81, 86, 239-44
200th Coast Artillery, 11, 52
Tulagi, 111

United Nations, 65
U.S. Forces in the Philippines (USFIP), 102
"urgent measures," 213

Vachon, Joseph P., Brigadier General, 85
VFW Post 673, 204
Vietnam, 207-09
Vigan, Luzon, 49, 50
Visayan Islands, 101
Vladivostok, 110
Voice of Freedom, 104

Wainwright, Jonathan "Skinny," Lieutenant General, 77, 101, 102, 103, 104, 118, 223, 237-38
Wake Is., 36, 45, 76, 110, 149, 232
Wakeman General Hospital, 185
War Dept., 36, 92, 102, 231, 236
Washington, D.C., 35, 41, 64, 91, 92, 101, 103, 163, 186, 189, 204
Waterford, Van, 138
Wells, Montgomery, 189
Whitcomb, Edgar D., Gov., 10, 202, 239
White, William H., 222
William B. Preston, USS (tender), 44
Williams, E. C., Colonel, 104
Willoughby, Charles A., Colonel, 95
Wilson, F. H., Lieutenant Colonel, 95
Wright, Orville, 222
Wright-Patterson Field, 191

Yokahama, 177

Zeros (fighters), 43, 68, 222, 248-49